ROSSLYN CHAPEL

THE MUSIC OF THE CUBES

THOMAS J. MITCHELL

diversions

First published in the United Kingdom by Diversions Books,
a division of Divine Art Ltd,
8 The Beeches, East Harlsey, Northallerton, DL6 2DJ

www.divine-art.com

Cover design by Stuart and Tommy Mitchell
Edited by Stephen Sutton and Typeset by Divine Art

British Library Cataloguing in Publication Data
available

ISBN: 0-9554629-0-8

978-0-9554629-0-0

The Author

Thomas J. Mitchell was born in 1932 in Lanarkshire, Scotland. He is a retired professional musician. Tommy played brass baritone in the Royal Air Force Iraq Command Military Band in the early 1950s. It was during this period that he became interested in pre-history while visiting many of the ancient sites in the Middle East. Tommy also played piano and organ in his career and made a study of the ancient diatonic scale and its relationships to sacred geometry and esoteric teachings. He became a Freemason in the early 1960s and gained access to information that had a bearing on his lifetime interest in the history of music and its relationship to classical architecture. It was this interest that led him in the late 1970s to the mystery of the cubes in Rosslyn Chapel and the possibility that music lay hidden in the arches.

TOMMY MITCHELL

This book describes the discovery of ancient music encoded in the stone carvings at Rosslyn Chapel, near Edinburgh, Scotland.

The resulting music is simple, haunting and beautiful.

THE ROSSLYN MOTET has been recorded for Diversions, a label of Divine Art Records. This CD, which also contains Thomas Mitchell's "Songs of the Chartres Labyrinth", is available from good record stores and websites worldwide or direct from the publisher's secure on-line store at:

www.divine-art.com

Diversions CD 24122

Contents

Acknowledgments

I should like to thank my family for their patience and support over the years while I pursued my quest for answers at Rosslyn Chapel; to my wife Margaret for patiently putting up with my idiosyncrasies while researching the cubes on our many visits to the Chapel, and in particular to my son Stuart who has created a very fine score and arranged the music of the cubes, to demonstrate the beautiful and haunting melodies that were realised from the cubes in the arches.

Also to Beth Fordyce for her invaluable help and advice in proof reading the manuscript, and for which help I am very grateful.

Tommy Mitchell

Preface

My journey to Rosslyn Chapel began in 1952 when I was serving in Iraq with the Royal Air Force. I was stationed 50 miles south west of Baghdad near Lake Habbaniyah. The ancient Sumerian city of Babylon was a mere 40 miles from our station and I was fortunate enough to have the opportunity to visit it. Knowing that it was pre-Christian by many thousands of years, I was truly amazed by the scale and the sophistication of the buildings that had been excavated.

The gateways to the city had also been excavated and partly refurbished. Finished in glazed coloured tiles, they depicted several types of animals. Most of all I was impressed by the inescapable sense of antiquity and I came away with a conviction that we in the west, with our technological civilization, had little or no idea regarding the Sumerians and how they lived. Their civilization flourished for thousands of years before our history had even begun. I came home after two years in Iraq with a firm aim to explore and study prehistory and also to find out just exactly what we are missing, both physically and spiritually, which was known by those civilisations and which made them so successful in their time.

The journey proved to be the journey of a lifetime and is still in progress! Many aspects are written here in the following chapters, and it is a surprising fact that the lines of inquiry led down many seemingly unrelated roads, but which eventually proved to be part of the bigger picture. At the time, I was too close to it to bring it into perspective or focus. A good analogy here would be to imagine a cartwheel with many spokes around the rim. Every spoke, although it starts from a different position on the rim, yet leads back to the axis. The axis contains the basic truth and from one point of view, it is the source from which the spokes emerge.

About 30 years ago I, as a musician, had realized from my experience and my studies that the diatonic musical scale—the basis of all music—was related by its mathematics and ratios, to the sacred geometry of architecture and art. I began to see the musical scale as a mirror of all creation and as time went on this conviction became the basis of my study of the seven wonders of the ancient world and the reason why they are still revered today as man's greatest achievements. My son Stuart and I collaborated on a suite for orchestra titled *The Seven Wonders of the Ancient World* and this brought me to the point where I began to see Rosslyn Chapel as the Eighth Wonder. I had researched the Chapel for a number of years from the viewpoint of a Freemason and from my earlier researches I had already pondered the cubes in the arches. This book takes the reader on a trip to the resolution of the decoding of the cubes and its relationship to the much wider area of spiritual evolution, which I believe William St Clair had in mind when he designed the Chapel. It is obvious to me that he had music very much in mind and must have known the relationship between music and sacred geometry, which may be the reason that he secreted the music of the Chapel in the arches between the pillars.

Tommy Mitchell
3/3/2006

Fig. 1:Ishtar Gate, Babylon

THE HOLY GRAIL

The search for a Holy Grail has kept men busy for centuries.
They search for the secret of Life,
The beginnings of the Universe,
Eternal Life,
Salvation.

But the search for a Holy Grail has missed the mark entirely.
The idea of a search is meant to guide us to the true Grail...Life.
One cannot search for Life,
Nor find a source for Life,
Within the confines of the physical universe.

Life is that infinite quality whose mere absence,
Would rob all things of their relevance and their meaning.
It is the invisible Creator,
On which all things rest,
And have their Being.

There is no location for Life,
There is no explanation for Life,
There is no substitute for Life,
It cannot be dissected nor duplicated,
Nor can it be contained within any thing,
Life is infinite... aware.
It is omnipresent and multi-dimensional,
Life IS...

Tommy Mitchell

Introduction
Rosslyn Chapel

Before we can understand the reasons why William St Clair built the Rosslyn Chapel on this particular site in 1446, and lavished so much care on its structure and decoration, we must first look further afield.

In medieval times, Rosslyn was the final stage for pilgrims on the long pilgrimage from St James Cathedral at Compostela in northern Spain, in seven stages via Notre Dame de Dalbade, Orléans Cathedral, Chartres Cathedral, Notre Dame de Paris, Amiens Cathedral and finally Rosslyn Chapel. The mystical number of seven represented the seven stages of the pilgrimage. In each case the association of the Cathedrals to the seven planets (as known in those days), each with its own unique spiritual signature, is significant. (See pages 7 and 8)

Pilgrims, wishing to complete their spiritual development and awaken their spiritual energies, undertook this strenuous journey, finally completing their goal on reaching Rosslyn, represented by Saturn. This was not originally a Christian pilgrimage, and the journey had been undertaken by Celtic pilgrims and Druids, who worshipped the Earth Goddess before the birth of Christianity. They journeyed from Spain to Scotland via the seven planetary oracles, associating the alignment of the spiritual awareness within themselves at each stage of the seven places of power.

The medieval Christian Church was an intolerant authority in Europe and after its suppression of the Templar order, the pilgrims had to disguise their journey as a series of Christian pilgrimages to the Cathedrals built on the seven sacred sites. Rosslyn Chapel is built on the place of power representing the Saturn oracle. It is here that the aesthetic and spiritual power of sacred music resides.

The mathematics of sacred geometry is common to both art in architecture and in the mathematics and construction of music and the diatonic scale. This being so, then by the laws of resonance the earth energies and cosmic energies can be focused and collected by the structures which mirror the mathematics and the resonant frequencies of the universal energies.

The earliest example is that of the Giza pyramid and it has been proven on many occasions over the years that potent energies exist and have strange effects within the pyramid structure.

It is therefore not a very great leap of faith to imagine, by the same mathematics and the laws of resonance, that sacred music could be encoded into the sacred geometry of such a building.

Pythagoras, in Greek times, said that the Diatonic scale was the mathematical representation of music and that all of life was a symphony of musical notes either in harmony or in disharmony. The diatonic scale represented Man and his environment as the micro-cosmos and the universe at large as the macro-cosmos.

As above — so below.

Fig.2: The Parthenon. It is the most important and characteristic monument of the ancient Greek civilization. It was dedicated to Athena Parthenos, the patron goddess of Athens. It was built between 447 and 438 B.C., and represents the iconic image of the ancient world and the beauty of architecture built to the divine proportions of sacred geometry.

Chapter 1
The Rosslyn Mysteries

There is a common mathematical bond between music as represented by the diatonic musical scale and sacred geometry, derived from gnosis and the seven planets of the ancient world. It has often been said that the medieval Cathedral, designed in relation to sacred geometry, is music embodied in stone. It is also the source of the idea of the music of the spheres. The most basic of those three ideas is music, which transcends the confusions of language and is understood and appreciated by all mankind.

Again, we find the mystical numbers recurring in the structure of music... the seven notes of the diatonic scale and the three modes of the structure, being rhythm, harmony and melody. It therefore follows that if designer William St. Clair decided to embody ancient secrets within the Chapel, he would both use sacred geometry in the carvings of the Chapel and carve sacred music into the arches using the mathematics and symbols common to both.

When the Chapel was being built, one has to remember that it was a time of great danger for anyone who opposed the medieval church with heretical ideas, and prior to this, the Knights Templar had been persecuted and disbanded by the political forces surrounding the church. William St Clair planned to enshrine the truths, which had been discovered in Jerusalem by the Templars, in the fabric of the Chapel within its sacred geometry and carvings. Perhaps the real treasures are truths, the sacred knowledge and history enshrined within the Chapel and which are there for those with eyes to see and an open mind to consider.

Part of that sacred knowledge and treasure is embodied in music and preserved in the arches behind the Master Mason and Apprentice pillars which are carved entirely with projecting cubes - each of which contains symbols - within which it is believed that musical notation is contained. On closer inspection, one can observe various carvings depicting figures holding a variety of musical instruments and at one point a figure is shown holding an open book with the written pages facing outwards. Those clues to the nature of the cubes confirm the idea that a sacred musical message is hidden therein.

A very great amount of trouble was taken to carve the numerous cubes and symbols and it seems to me that if it were merely to act as a decoration then it need not have been so detailed or complicated. That in itself was an indicator that something special had been embodied in the arches.

The fact that the Chapel contains references to Freemasonry, as in the Apprentice and Master Mason's pillars above which the arches and cubes are carved, also tells me that there is very much more to Rosslyn Chapel than a Christian place of worship. The Templar Knights of St John allegedly brought back, from the near east, ancient pre-Christian knowledge which was later embodied in the Freemasonry movement, and this also tells me that the Chapel has a much more interesting story to tell us from its proportions and carvings. There are numerous books on the history of the Chapel for anyone who wishes to pursue this aspect.

Fig. 3: Rosslyn Chapel

THE MOON.

MERCURY.

VENUS.

THE SUN.

MARS.

JUPITER.

SATURN.

The seven planetary squares are associated with the seven stages of the pilgrimage from St James of Compostela, represented by the Moon, to Rosslyn Chapel at the end of the route, represented by Saturn. Each square is numbered and in each case adds up horizontally, vertically and diagonally to make the mystical number of each of the planets.

Saturn, representing Rosslyn Chapel, has nine numbers and each line adds up to fifteen, being the number for Saturn. It is these mystical numbers, when extended via sacred geometry, which imparts to the buildings their sacred proportions, which are associated with each of the planets.

Music in the ancient world was closely related to measure, the lengths of strings and of wind instruments representing certain measures. These same measures were used by architects who planned the proportions of their buildings by the ratios of diatonic music. The Renaissance architect, Leon Battista Alberti, wrote that "the numbers, by means of which the agreement of sounds affects our ears with delight, are the very same which please our eyes and our minds."

The Diatonic Scale and the Planetary Oracles

The Diatonic musical scale encapsulates the sacred mathematics and qualities of the Planetary Oracles and each of these qualities can be mirrored by music.

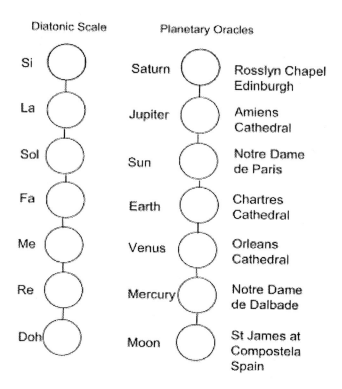

Diatonic Scale	Planetary Oracles	
Si	Saturn	Rosslyn Chapel Edinburgh
La	Jupiter	Amiens Cathedral
Sol	Sun	Notre Dame de Paris
Fa	Earth	Chartres Cathedral
Me	Venus	Orleans Cathedral
Re	Mercury	Notre Dame de Dalbade
Doh	Moon	St James at Compostela Spain

Each of the stages undertaken by the pilgrims on their spiritual journey from St James of Compostela to Rosslyn Chapel predates the Christian era and had much more to do with so-called Pagan beliefs than the Christian doctrine. The Christian church merely overlaid the 'places of power' with their own Cathedrals and absorbed the Pagan pilgrimage into their own doctrinal teachings.

Chapter 2
Decoding the Cubes

To approach the problem of attempting to make sense of the cubes and their symbols one has to make certain assumptions. First of all, we can never know what was in William St. Clair's mind or what his actual goal was in designing the cubes in the arches above the pillars. After 500 years, all we have to go on is mainly the hard evidence of the actual carvings and an attempt to make sense of them. Therefore, the results of any of our efforts will be to a great extent an interpretation based on the little historical evidence that we have and, of course, a degree of intuition based on the hard evidence.

For this reason I decided to approach the problem from the point of view of music. As a professional musician, I have made a lifetime study of the diatonic musical scale and its associated mathematics and history. I knew that if the cubes did conceal music then the symbols would reflect the logic and the phrasing of musical expression via the diatonic scale, which is an ancient esoteric principle and it is central to the entire history of esoteric teaching.

One of the assumptions I made was that musical notation was not widespread in the mid-15th century; there was some notation, usually handwritten, but music and musical tradition was mainly passed on orally. The modern musical stave was just beginning to appear (see page 16 and Appendix). William St. Clair, if he required to conceal the music in secret notational form, would have to devise a system using symbols to represent the musical notation, and which could be carved in stone. Then the cubes would be arranged across the arches in recognisable patterns and groupings to simulate musical phrasing that could be recognised by a musician who took the time and effort to decode them.

The most difficult part of the exercise was to identify the numbers of different symbols and note their repetition, grouping and positions on the arches. The arches were photographed and a layout of the cubes was drawn up. Each of the symbols was quantified and repeating symbols were plotted in their positions in the arches. This was a time consuming operation but very necessary to identify the groupings.

Many cubes had more than one symbolic design plus the ends of the cubes had smaller markings. These markings gave clues to the note values and rests and, as I proceeded with the interpretation, the musical phrases which were already emerging helped to confirm that this was the case. Over a period of time, there was inevitably a great deal of trial, error and use of intuition, which in the end led to an acceptable interpretation.

Regarding pitch, this was ascertained by identifying the A note on the diatonic scale which vibrates at 435Hz. This is the ancient version of concert pitch which is a relatively recent innovation. Many experts believe that the 435 version gives purer and more natural tones, but the new concert pitch of 440Hz was instituted to suit modern orchestral instruments. It was a simple exercise, then, to read back to the *keynote* of the scale as provided by the ending cadence, and from that point the various pitches of the notes could be matched up to the symbols.

This was done was by first identifying the *cadence* at the end of each arch. A cadence is a sequence of musical notes and chords which were commonly used in music over the centuries to 'end off' a piece, and this always terminated by resolving to the keynote, thus leaving a feeling of completeness or 'resolution' which means, "to conclude concordantly." Having found the keynote, this was then applied to the start of each arch and I could begin to translate the cubes into a musical score.

We can use an analogy here, which will help to illustrate this process. The man given credit for decoding the Rosetta Stone was Jean Francois Champollion, a French scholar. Using his knowledge of Greek and Coptic, and the Egyptian language of his time, Champollion was able to determine the meanings of the hieroglyphics at the top of the stone. His 'keynote' was his discovery of the *cartouche* symbol which is an oblong figure enclosing characters expressing royal or divine names in Egyptian hieroglyphics.

Champollion at one point was completely at a loss regarding the hieroglyphs until he recognised that the cartouche was a figure that was repeated frequently. While examining one of these figures, he suddenly recognised the symbol for Rameses, an early Pharaoh, and realised the connection between this and other symbols used in the hieroglyphics. It was the breakthrough he had been waiting for, and from that point he never looked back. This is a typical example of a key moment in the solution to a mystery, when one element in the puzzle becomes the key point that connects and resolves the mysteries of the remaining symbols.

At this point, it was knowledge of music, musical composition and a modicum of intuition that completed the puzzle, and the beautiful haunting melodies began to emerge from the stone cubes. It was impossible to doubt, as the music emerged, that the solution to the mystery of the cubes had been solved. If it had been random sounds from an error of logic, there would have been no musical continuity or form to the sounds that emerged, but what did emerge was very much of its time and in the nature of musical structures of the 15th century. Here was the music laid to rest in the arches in the mid-1400s and frozen in stone, resurrected after 500 years and designed to resonate with the sacred geometry built into the Chapel, for reasons that we are still not aware!

In all of the speculation regarding the Holy Grail being hidden in the Chapel, I cannot but feel that the music and its interaction with the sacred geometry may be at least part of what the Grail represents.

Besides the cubes, there are several carvings associated with music at the top of the pillars where the arches and cubes terminate. These represent cherub figures playing medieval instruments. The instruments were a clue to the fact of the music secreted in the cubes and one figure in particular is holding an open book with the pages facing outward as if to suggest melodies in the arches. The instruments include a lute, bagpipes, organetto, flute or pipe, and drum, all of which were instruments of the period. This would also have included a choir, as the voice was the most common 'instrument' then in use.

I worked very much from the diatonic musical scale as the starting point as it was the music within the cubes that provided the final proof that I was on the right track.

The Proof - Music in the Arches of Rosslyn Chapel

At the east end of the chapel is a beautiful arrangement of 14 arches and along each of these arches are 213 cubes protruding from a 'stem' all the way from north to south. At the beginning of each arch there are angels/musicians each playing a musical instrument. At the start of the first arch is a lute player, then a violinist, bagpiper, choral singers, flute-player, drummer and finally a figure with an instrument called an Organetto. In short, it is a standard medieval orchestra and choir with a score to perform, represented by cubes carved with esoteric symbols instead of our accepted modern notational symbols. The fact that the musicians are there at the start of each arch points significantly to the arrangement of cubic symbols being a musical sequence performed by each musician.

There are a number of academic musical aspects within the sequence of the cubes which indicate the arches as being the 'staves' containing a musical arrangement, for example where two separate arches arrive upon the same cadence at the same ends of their arches and the curious harmonic combining of the simultaneous performance of two different arches which creates a simple harmonic and melodic counterpoint, clearly indicative of 15th Century Motet compositional development.

Each cube reappears in a regular fashion, sometimes at different intervals in time, and occasionally with repeated notes in succession. For example, the tambour (percussion) was one of the first and simplest sequences to decode since a tambour emits one single note (beat) and requires no alteration in pitch, therefore it made perfect sense to me that when notating for a percussion instrument of this type, a composer would use one single line of the stave or one single pitch (or cubic symbol) to notate its part in the score.

Interestingly, the fact that all of these geometric symbols on the cubes are collectively found under the wave form phenomena of Cymatics merely confirms that the arrangement of cubes are in fact musical notes and I believe it is beyond coincidence that Cymatics symbols match the Rosslyn Cube symbols and are the by-product of the frequency of diatonic musical pitches and their effect upon nature. All things considered, this means that the designer of the symbolic notational system within the chapel was aware of this science at least 250 years before its initial discovery, or 're-discovery', by Margaret Watts Hughes in the 1800s. We shall discuss the Cymatics symbols and their significance more fully in the following chapters.

The fact is that the cubes demonstrate universal laws such as the law of resonance which is known to have been an integral part of the Hindu, Arabic and Egyptian cultures. The mathematics of the sacred geometry is common to both art in architecture and in the mathematics and construction of music and the diatonic scale. This being so, then by the laws of resonance the earth energies and cosmic energies can be focused and collected by the structures which mirror the mathematics and the resonant frequencies of the universal energies.

The earliest example is that of the Great Pyramid at Giza and it has been proven on many occasions over the years that potent energies exist and have strange effects within the pyramid structure. It is therefore not a very great leap of faith to imagine that by the same mathematics and the laws of resonance, that sacred music could be encoded into the sacred geometry of such a building as Rosslyn Chapel. The final result is an artistic bridge connecting the 15th century to the 21st century by way of haunting and exciting music hidden away for so long.

The decoding of the symbols on the cubes had a great similarity to solving a crossword puzzle. When you work out the answer to the first clue, you are well on the way to solving the subsequent clues. In each case, the answers to the subsequent clues had to enmesh with the previous answers as in a crossword and this in itself provided a fail-safe method of knowing that I had the correct solution. The music hidden in the cubes has lain undisturbed for the best part of 500 years and many people have written about it and puzzled over the symbolism of the cubes. The clues were there for those to see if they had approached it from a musical direction rather than a symbolic direction. In other words, it took a musician with knowledge of the music in stone and the ancient diatonic scale to decode the secrets of the cubes.

At this point, the music was scored for choir and medieval instruments, and produced a very beautiful and compelling arrangement of the musical interpretation of the cubes, which I named "The Rosslyn Motet." The music was recorded at Rosslyn in June 2006 by a splendid group of singers and specialist instrumentalists and has been released on CD, along with another composition of mine entitled "Songs of the Chartres Labyrinth", by Divine Art Records.

Fig. 4 : Chartres Cathedral labyrinth. This was meant to be walked in the past as a pilgrimage for repentance.

Chapter 3
The Fibonacci Series of Numbers

At this point I would like to outline some of the mathematical relationships between the diatonic scale and sacred geometry which is the source of the saying that "sacred geometry is music carved in stone." The very best and simplest way is by using a simple series of numbers called 'the Fibonacci series'. All of the great architecture of the past can be defined and explained using this simple series of numbers, which also defines the Golden Section or Divine Proportion used in the great buildings of the golden era of architecture starting with the great pyramid at Giza in Egypt.

Leonardo Fibonacci was born in Pisa, in what is now Italy, in 1170 and went on to be a great mathematician who found favour at the court of Frederick II. He is perhaps best known for a simple series of numbers, introduced in his book, *Liber abaci* and later named the *Fibonacci numbers*. The discovery of this series of numbers is probably one of the most significant events in the history of mathematics and its direct bearing on the relationship between music and sacred geometry, that is the foundation for an incredible mathematical relationship behind **phi**.

The series of numbers begins with 0 and 1. The simple rule thereafter is to add the previous two numbers to obtain the next in the series.

e.g. 1+2 = 3   2+3 = 5   3+5 = 8 thus giving us the following sequence 1, 2, 3, 5, 8, 13, 21, 34, 55, 89, 144, 233, 377, 610, 987, etc.

The ratio of each successive pair of numbers in the series approximates phi (1.618. . .) as 5 divided by 3 is 1.666..., and 8 divided by 5 is 1.60. In formal mathematics, this is termed a converging series and has great significance in geometry and physics. The table below shows how the ratios of the successive numbers in the Fibonacci series converge on phi.

After the 40th number in the series, the ratio is accurate to fifteen decimal places. How did this come about? At this time in the 15th century, mathematical competitions and challenges were quite common. In 1225 Fibonacci took part in a tournament at Pisa ordered by Frederick II, the Holy Roman Emperor. One of the problems set to the competitors was: Beginning with a single pair of rabbits, if every month each *productive* pair bears a new pair, which becomes productive when they are one month old, how many rabbits will there be after *n* months? The short answer is that, as a result of solving this problem, Fibonacci gave us the Fibonacci series of numbers that have served us well to this day!

The Golden Section or Divine Proportion

A special value, closely related to the Fibonacci Series, is called the *golden section*. This value is obtained by taking the ratio of successive terms in the Fibonacci Series.

The Golden Section is also known as the Golden Mean, Golden Ratio and Divine Proportion. It is a ratio or proportion derived from the Fibonacci series and defined by the number phi (= 1.618033988749895...) The result is a mathematical explanation of why the Golden Section is the ideal proportion for architecture, art and music - why it is so pleasing to the eye and harmonious to the ear. It is this particular ratio that defines sacred geometry and its relationship to music and the diatonic scale.

The ancient Greek mathematicians recognized phi as a significant value and Greek architects used the ratio *1:phi* as an integral part of their designs, the most famous of which is the Parthenon in Athens. The Renaissance artists knew it as the Divine Proportion, and collectively it was understood as the sacred geometry, which was used to design the ancient monuments of the seven wonders of the world.

Chapter 4
The Diatonic Musical Sscale

When I began to study music in depth at college, the course began with practical demonstrations which involved setting up the original Pythagoras experiments using a meter-long string between two pegs, which when plucked showed in graphic detail the loops or wavelength of the string. At either side of the loops was a 'still point' or 'node' over which a thread could be carefully placed and which stayed there without any movement. If moved along the string marginally, it would fly off as it contacted the vibrations of the string.

By lightly touching the node points with a card, one could hear the harmonics or 'partials' into which the string was divided. In this way, we experimented with the harmonics to find the perfect intervals and thus we could find and measure the ratios of the perfect fourth and fifth tones. This was a practical demonstration of the Fibonacci mathematics series and how those intervals were derived from the maths. (see below)

Probably one of the most interesting connections with the Fibonacci series is the construction and the ratios of the ancient diatonic musical scale based on the Fibonacci numbers and which is the basis of all music including the modern chromatic scale.

Using the following numbers, we derive the interval ratios of the scale. Fibonacci numbers: $1 : 1 : 2 : 3 : 5 : 8 : 13 : 21$

The ascending series forms a smooth series of even musical intervals:

$1 : 1$ Unison
$3 : 2$ Perfect 5th
$8 : 5$ Minor 6th
$21 : 13$ Minor 6th
⇩

Infinity : Harmonic 6th

The series will progress to infinity, always attempting to form a harmonic sixth. This interval does not exist and is non-perceptible as it represents perfect unity. When the series is reversed it forms enharmonic musical intervals:

21 : 13   Minor 6th
13 : 8   Minor 6th
 5 : 3   Major 6th
 2 : 1   Octave

Fibonacci sequences appear in nature in biological settings, such as the branching patterns of ferns, grasses and flowers, branching in bushes and trees, the arrangement of pines on a pine cone, seeds on a raspberry, spiral patterns in horns and shells, each being a Fibonacci number. One could say that natural creation is also based on this series of numbers and the golden mean or divine proportions.

The above connections, showing the relationship between the mathematics of the musical scale, the golden section and the Fibonacci series of numbers, make the most important connection between the sacred geometry of ancient buildings and the diatonic musical scale; both are based on the same ratios and numbers derived from the Fibonacci series. This is the source of the statement that sacred geometry is 'music in stone'.

The perfect proportions and the beauty of early Greek Temples and medieval Cathedrals bear this out. The acoustics present in Cathedrals built to the proportions of the Golden Mean provide an enhanced sound when listening to music played in a Cathedral, producing an unforgettable experience when they combine in the high arches of the Cathedral.

This mathematical relationship is inherent in all of Nature and appears to be the basis of creation as it is shared by flora and fauna alike. The Fibonacci series of numbers and its ratios can be said to be the perfect and most pleasing to the eye and the ideal shape for all of creation.

Chapter 5
The Discovery of a Three Note Cipher

When I was satisfied with the music and with the pitches of the symbols in place, I now turned to the carvings of the array of musicians running from south to north along the three dominant pillars, to accurately define what these 15th century instruments are, in order to produce an authentic recording of the Motet. All of the musicians are very well preserved and contain a great deal of detail pertaining to each instrument's tunings, size and logical performance position. Every musician is performing in the most natural and academically correct performance position. In fact, the detail is so clear in most figures that it made the task of identifying the instruments very easy indeed and even gave me an accurate estimation of what note ranges were possible for each instrument during this period of history.

William St. Clair had gone to a great deal of trouble and effort to make us aware of the complexities, design and version of each instrument. The Lute player, for example, explicitly displays the number of pegs on the head of the fret board allowing us to understand how many strings were possible, and the instrument's lowest and highest note range. The same applies to the fiddle player and the manner and technique in which the wind instruments are performing.

So far, we had identified the Lowland Bagpipes, Fife and Tabor, Fiddle, Recorder, Mute Cornett, Organetto, Renaissance Lute and Tin Whistle. The choir seems to be self explanatory, as they are portrayed as figures singing from a book to a text (we will elaborate upon the choice of text in Chapter 9). Now we have identified all but one instrument.

This figure/musician is second from the right on The Apprentice Pillar and the cubes emanating above him declare the second theme that appears in the piece. It also contains an opening sequence of symbols revealing a recurring melodic *motif* that appears frequently throughout the piece.

At first sight, the instrument in the carving looks like a Psaltery or Dulcimer; however, the instrument that the angel is (supposedly) performing upon, has been specifically carved to show a five-stringed lyre-type instrument being played in a position in which it would be completely impossible to perform correctly. Given the fact that the instrument has been tilted forward on its side, pointing away from the performer, it thus places the strings out of his line of sight. In addition, his hands are at opposite ends of the string, and therefore he is performing upon the 'tightest' point of the string creating what could be termed as nothing less than a dull 'thud' in the performance. This is totally inconsistent with the detail of all the other musician carvings, since even the Lute player has his fingers over the exact notes that he about to play.

I was convinced for months that this was a Psaltery he was playing and had found the notion of the sound of the Psaltery amongst the sound-mix as an attractive addition to the tonal make-up. But things just did not add up this particular musician.

Firstly, there are no pegs showing on the ends of the strings to adjust the length of the strings to tune them (as there is in the Lute and Fiddle carvings).

Secondly, in all my years of music, I have never seen a lyre, psaltery or dulcimer played in this manner, with the performer's thumbs resting on the top of the instrument doing nothing (which is quite contrary to string performance since plucking with the thumbs is a foundational element of technique) and the instrument's face is turned away from the performer who then has to 'guess' where and what string to pluck in order to produce the music. Some people believe this is a type of Organetto, not the portative kind as shown in the sixth carving (*fig. 13*), but of a more solid type, but this concept still does not fit in with the detail of the other instruments. **In my opinion, it is not an instrument.**

On closer inspection (zooming in at only 200X with a good graphics program), you can see with greater detail that the 'musician' is in fact a singer (*fig. 5*), a counter-tenor by the look of his build and stature. In addition, he is leaning on a 'rostrum' or 'podium' with his mouth open projecting his vocal power in his expression and deliberation of intention. He is not aware he is performing upon an instrument but he is aware of the position of his fingers.

So, if this is it not an instrument, why did they carve the five lines and spaces that are cunningly disguised as strings? In my opinion and that of my son Stuart, the musician is a 'decoy' that subtly points out the 'key' to 70% of the content in the music. This is not an instrument but a **stave of music** carved on the front of a rostrum and the 'singer's' fingertips are pointing precisely at the notes he is singing in the sequence of cubes rising in an arch above him (see *fig. 5*).

Fig. 5 : A Lyre, an Organ or a Psaltery, or is it
a musical stave this figure is pointing at ?

To a musician, an arrangement of five lines and four spaces is like the alphabet to a writer or a colour pallet to a painter or the Periodic Table to a scientist. It is the fundamental of music notation, which was invented by an Italian Monk named Guido d'Arezzo (995-1050 A.D.). He invented the system of staff-notation by combining a four-line stave with the first form of notes known as 'neumes'. He was educated by and became a member of the Benedictine Order in the monastery of St. Maur des Fosses, near Paris. He introduced a way freezing music in time and in a way in which singers would refrain from improvising and glorifying the liturgical melodies which were sacred up until then, and only passed on orally or misread in the 'neumes' which was a highly specialist art form to possess at the time. By the time Rosslyn Chapel was built, the universally accepted standard for staff notation was five lines, though four lines for plainchant. There had been variants of six-line and even eight-line staffs for various instruments throughout the centuries but five lines became the norm during the 1400s. Interestingly, standard notation was originally developed for use with human voice.

Further investigation into the figure (*fig. 6*) shows that the tips of his fingers are placed strategically upon the stave at three specific points. B, C and A. From the side (*fig. 5*) he appears to be curling his fingers of his left hand to put them in place whilst the fingers of the right hand seem relaxed when reaching down to the B line.

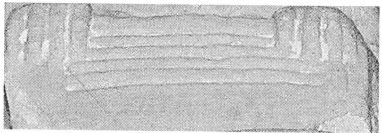

Fig. 6 – The fingers are not symmetrical but touching 3 different points/notes on a 5-line stave. Notice that the 'strings' have no tuning pegs!

This was just one of the first realisations in deciding this was not an instrument but a singer and that he was quite evidently pointing to the first three notes he was performing, telling us the identity of the first three cube symbols in the sequence which runs along the arch above this angel's head.

The second realisation was astounding! It immediately occurred to me when I saw the notes he was indicating was that "they appear to be the notes of the opening themes" and to my astonishment, they were exactly that (see *figs. 7 and 8*). The pitch of the notes I assigned using the Cymatics/Voice Pattern formula were (according to this angel's fingering) 100% right. Three notes correct out of three. But the interesting thing was that between the three symbols pointed out by the angel, they account for 113 of the 215 cubes. That is around 55% of the entire work. So it began to dawn on me that if the cymatics formula was correct as this showed, then the formula must be valid throughout the entire work. It was almost as if this figure and stave was verifying the music and the cymatics formula at the same time. But why is he only giving us three notes and not more?

I believe the designer wanted us to apply the cymatics knowledge to the sequence of cubes. This appears to be the total amount of verification and only clue we are 'allowed'. If he were to simply offer up all the notes, there would be no reason to carve such elaborate geometric symbols on the cube faces. Had we discovered the five-stave 'melodic cipher' *before* the application of Cymatics, Voice Patterns and Chladni patterns, we would still have at least 45% of the cubes to define and that is why there has to be a formula to break the symbols and this carving is telling you (if the notes match) that you have found it. In many ways, the cymatics musical/pattern vocabulary is far more sophisticated, visual and accurate to natural music than the restrictive five-line stave of Western notation. (A great many experimental musicians and musicologists using other systems claim that standard notation is less than ideally suited to instrumental music). It is also interesting to note that he has managed to combine within the same musical setting a standard musical notation system and a

24

natural alternative notation that clearly works as a system due to my interpretation of the symbols using the cymatics formula.

I have to ask myself, is it too much of a coincidence that Cymatics is so closely related to music and the patterns and forms of its production are mirrored heavily in every one of the thirteen symbols on Rosslyn Chapel's ceiling? And yet again here we find a standard five-line stave only eight inches away from a Cymatics pattern with a carved angel's fingers verifying the pattern's pitch? And the pitches are correct for each one? There have been many 'happy coincidences' along the way on this journey but this didn't feel like a coincidence. There was a feeling of inevitability about the 'cipher', as if it had been waiting to be discovered, and to serve its purpose by delivering its musical message to the finder.

> "If thoust can comprehend these things, thoust know enough"- William St Clair

Since the very first moment I began my research at Rosslyn regarding the cubes, I was always certain that whoever decided to contain a musical piece in code, would leave a 'cipher', 'primer' or 'key' which contained a clue to the discovery of the notes. It is almost as if he knew someday someone would pay close inspection to the detail on this particular carved angel and thereby eliminate it as an actual instrument, thus seeing the musical truth beyond the decoy. Like all good primers, a large portion of the work has been staring everyone in the face for centuries and by directing this central angel on The Apprentice Pillar to point at the leading notes, we can now hear the true music that the designer intended.

Here we can see that the hands and the fingers have been very carefully carved, in this instance alone, as the hands on the other musician figures are plain standard carvings, where the fingers are all the same length. In this case above, one can see that the figure's hands have been carved to show exactly which lines and spaces the Angel is pointing to. This is no coincidence and I am convinced that this particular figure has been placed in that position as a major clue to the function of the cubes and the musician carvings.

As there is a certain likeness between the carved angel with the stave and the medieval psaltery, I did some research and I quote here from an article on the psaltery by Rosemary Ingram of *Psaltery Dreams*, in which she notes that there is a strong tradition that the musical stave was derived from this instrument in the way she describes. This fits in very well with my interpretation of the carved angel and the stave.

A Brief History of the Psaltery

"The psaltery is a type of medieval zither. It is an ancient instrument is seen in many forms (trapezoidal, wing-shaped and hog-nosed to name a few). The instrument's name may have derived from the Greek psallein, meaning 'plucked with fingers'. Early versions were simply a wooden board with gut strings stretched between pegs. According to historic sources, metal strings were made of bronze. Compared to steel, bronze strings gave the instrument a bell-like sound. The strings are normally plucked with a plectrum, pick, or the fingernails. The player performed with the instrument on the lap or on a table, or in front of the chest held with a strap around his neck if movement was needed.

The plucked psaltery began in the Middle East, around the Mesopotamia area, where Iran and Iraq are today. It is thought to be about three thousand years old, only slightly younger than the oldest stringed instrument, the harp. Crusaders are believed to have brought it back to Europe although there is no way to positively prove.

Southern Europe, influenced by Moorish Spain, preferred the trapezoidal psaltery with three or four strings to a note. Northern psalteries tended to be triangular or wing-shaped and single or double-strung.

Like most other instruments of the time, the psaltery had no specific repertory, but was used to play whatever music the occasion demanded. It was referred to frequently in lists of musicians and instruments and in the art of the time. The psaltery was widely used until about 1500. After the 1500s it could not cope well with the chromaticism of the Renaissance era, so was used less as time passed. It is thought that the psaltery evolved into the harpsichord, hammered dulcimer and then went through mechanization process producing the pianoforte, which became, of course, the piano. The psaltery is the cornerstone upon which the most commonly played stringed instrument, the piano, is built.

Due to its reference in the bible and its ancient history, some scholars believe, the psaltery like the harp were acceptable for ladies of court to play. Psaltery music has its own interesting story. Approximately two hundred years after its arrival in Europe, someone figured out that if they made marks on a material thin enough to slide under the strings, they would not have to remember the music being played.

Original psaltery music, some of which has survived, fits under the strings similar to modern psaltery music. The big difference between the old and new music is that in the old music, all of the strings are completely drawn in. Knowing that the modern musical staff arose approximately one hundred years after written psaltery music, music historians believe that one day someone looked at the notations on lines for the psaltery music and figured out that if they used the spaces in between the scale could be compressed and, therefore, useful for instruments with larger range.

In other words, though it cannot be proven, it is a logical assumption that not only did psalteries spawn pianos, but also begat the entire method of music notation (sheet music) used by all instruments and performers in the modern world."

(from an article by Rosemary Ingram)

This goes some way to validating my first assumption that this particular carving is a major clue that the angel is indicating a musical stave and pointing to the first three notes of the Motet.

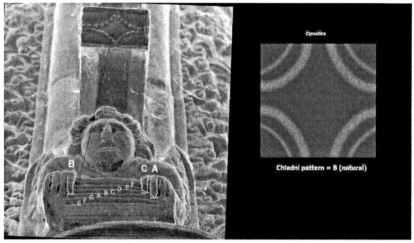

Fig. 7: The stave superimposed on the 'angel' and Chladni pattern corresponding to the first 'note' cube above.

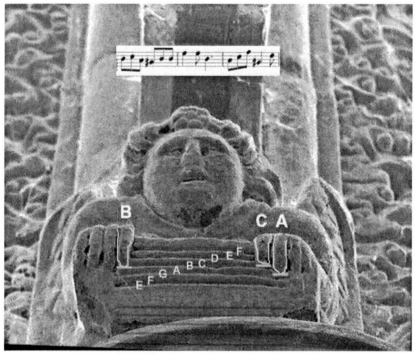

Fig. 8: The beginning of the score of the Motet, showing the first three notes indicated by the Angel.

Chapter 6
The Cubes and their Symbols

The greatest challenge of the entire project has been the unravelling of the pitches and the symbols carved into the faces of the cubes. If you can unlock the pitches with a formula, you can hear the melodic content of the sequence. I will break down the whole score for you now:

There are 213 surviving cubes attached to stems that emanate from each arch; each arch generally contains up to eight or nine cubes before it joins the central pendant arch meeting point that breaks the music into sections. There are smaller arch groups with lines of five, six or seven-note refrains to perform, and there are even arches with ten notes. There were originally 215 cubes but two have disappeared over the years due to vandalism (though there are other stories that could explain their disappearance, which go beyond the scope and subject of this guide). However, one of the lost cubes is on the percussion/Tabor Drum part and is amongst an array of repeated symbols, so it seems highly unlikely, given the system and instrument, that this cube symbol could be anything else than the same as the others. The second cube was not so easy to decide upon but having already built up a familiarity with the melodic progression in the writing, it was possible to read what potential symbol it could be using my musical instinct and examining the cadence patterns of the symbols throughout the score. Unless of course, it was a completely different symbol from the six basic patterns I had to work with.

Each cube contains a pattern of which there are six basic designs and a number of variations based on three of them. The symbols are all geometric in their shape and design, there are diamonds, and hexagons, flower shapes, crosses and squares turned on their sides with circles in the middle.

To me the real challenge was to find those symbols collectively "under one roof" and this began a ten-year mission to find their counterparts somewhere in the world: - in a book, in images, symbolic text or paintings. I even looked into Cuneiform text but to no avail. I did find them sometimes individually in the symbolism of Alchemy and Gnosticism but these areas never gave me any leads nor any more than a couple of the symbols to go on.

After many years of research with no real connection having been made, there was one avenue that I had not fully investigated; an unusual and highly undervalued science, which was named Cymatics in 1924 by Dr Hans Jenny, but which was first discovered and experimented with in 1725 by Ernst Chladni. (This date is one of the reasons that I left this subject to last since this science was (apparently) discovered at least 300 years after the design of Rosslyn. So it seemed highly unlikely to me that knowledge of this science would have been held by the designer of the Rosslyn cube music).

Nevertheless, extensive study and research into this sound-wave phenomenon proved to be the 'under one roof' scenario that I had been looking for. Every pattern that I found produced by those 'pure notes' mirrored in every detail the six basic patterns on the Rosslyn cubes, as illustrated in *Fig. 9*. Before we go on, I will give you a brief overview of the historical application of Cymatics and how these patterns are produced, by using an unbelievably simple apparatus that could have been invented at any other time in history.

The first experiments involving waveform patterns were performed and recorded by Ernest Chladni, an 18th century scientist, and this led to further experimentation in the 19th Century by Margaret Watts Hughes, a singer and amateur scientist. Incredibly, the apparatus used by each of these groundbreaking enthusiasts on this subject produce similar patterns, and the higher the pitch, the more complex the patterns and forms become. Chladni used a glass plate with fine sand strewn across it and 'stopped' or dampened the plate at various points then vibrated the glass with a violin bow, during which the sand, 'excited' by the frequency of the vibration (note/pitch) produced a geometric pattern, symbol or signature. Margaret Watts Hughes used a method/instrument she invented named the Eidophone, basically a 'flower pot' with a hole in it and she stretched Indian rubber over the top to act as a diaphragm, onto which she scattered fine sand. She would sing a very controlled note of definite amplitude and pitch to produce intriguing forms/patterns extraordinarily similar to those which Chladni had brought forth but with her voice. Mrs Watts Hughes's observations and patterns are in my opinion the closest examples there are to the Rosslyn Chapel symbols.

The later experiments by Swiss medical doctor and natural scientist, Hans Jenny (1904-1972) investigate these phenomena in even greater detail using crystal oscillators to generate a pure tone using a machine he himself invented, called a Tonoscope. Dr Jenny named this new area of research 'cymatics', which comes from the Greek word *kyma*, meaning 'wave'. Cymatics could be translated as: the study of how vibrations generate and influence patterns, shapes and moving processes.

Even though Dr Jenny's experiments used a higher and more efficient technology than his predecessors, the outcome of all the experiments over a three hundred year period, produced broadly the same (geometric) results. In all, the effect of the pitch and amplitude of a note universally creates the same *fundamental* pattern even under different conditions, materials and apparatus.

One of the Margaret Watts Hughes experiments in 1825 that intrigued me was when she began to apply powder with colour pigments, such as yellow, blue and red, where she found that the colour powders would arrange themselves into specific areas and patterns due to the frequency of the note applied. The note is simply vibrating in sympathy with the frequency (waveform) of the colour itself.

It would be extremely interesting to have had the opportunity of asking these pioneers of waveform vibration what their conclusions regarding the symbols on the Rosslyn Chapel cubes would have suggested. I feel with great certainty that they would have been remarkably surprised and intrigued to be confronted with an array of symbols that, in reality, had obviously been explored and discovered at least two centuries before their own discoveries and experimentations. If only Ernst Chladni or Margaret Watts Hughes had visited Rosslyn Chapel during their lifetime, we may have heard the music that those symbols

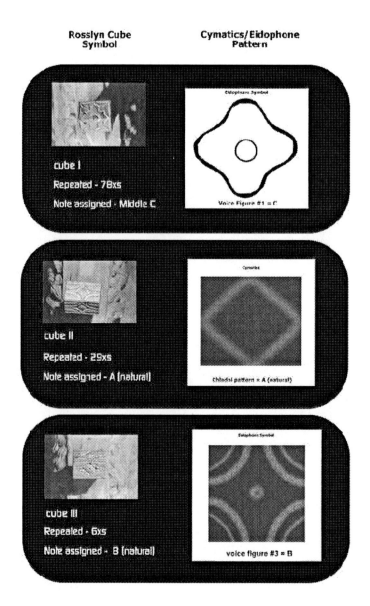

Fig. 9. This is a break down of three of the cube symbols and its corresponding pattern in the form of Cymatics. Once the note that produces the pattern in Cymatics or Eidophone voice figures is applied to each individual cube in the sequence of arches, a melodic structure reveals itself. This system (or formula as I like to call it) did not produce just random musical 'jargon' but a coherent and convincing musical and harmonic structure that sounded close to that which I had already uncovered, using a purely musical, academic and instinctive approach.

produce, in order of their sequence, at least 200 years ago. However, I have applied the system to the cubes and believe that this is the music that was intended by its creator.

Interestingly, the fact that all of these geometric symbols on the cubes are collectively found under the wave form phenomena of Cymatics merely confirms that the arrangement of cubes are in fact musical notes and I believe it is beyond coincidence that Cymatics symbols match the Rosslyn Cube symbols and are the by-product of the frequency of diatonic musical pitches and their effect upon nature. All things considered, this means that the designer of the symbolic notational system within the chapel was aware of this science at least 250 years before its initial discovery, or potential "re-discovery," by Ernst Chladni in the 18th Century.

If you begin to think about Cymatics as musical vibration upon the world of nature, you begin to see the patterns emerging in a bigger picture and even in a macro-cosmic way. Cymatics is present all around us, it always has been and it has been expressed and utilised for over 2000 years within Vedic and Hindu meditation and chant. They claim they are "channelling and patterning their energies up and down the lines of frequency using specific frequency vibrations (specific note pitches depending on the meditation) produced by their voice and body resonance". Chanting the word 'OM' in F# resonates your energies into the Earth frequency while other notes and tones serve other energy patterns for healing and spiritual cleansing of the aura.

There was also an interesting discovery made during the experiments of Dr Hans Jenny when be reported in his book 'Cymatics' that when the vowels of the ancient languages of Hebrew and Sanskrit were pronounced into his Tonoscope, the sand took the shape of the 'written' symbols for each of the vowels; our modern languages however did not produce the same phenomena. This could mean that the original ancient languages were born out of knowledge of sound and vibration and its healing/therapeutic properties.

Recent Cymatics experiments performed on the Sarcophagus in The Great Pyramid at Giza by acoustical physics and sound engineer John Reid may confirm this. He explains in an interview that while firing note frequencies across the membrane stretched over the top of the sarcophagus for the first time, to his astonishment the sand was producing patterns he had never seen before in any other cymatics experiments; the sand was organising itself into well known Egyptian hieroglyphs. This is because of the properties of the quartz crystals within the granite of the sarcophagus itself allow the box to make its own sound and generate its own frequencies. Each hieroglyph that was produced by John (over twenty of them) has found its way into the Egyptian language by the vibration of sound. This also means that if you were reading hieroglyphics you would also be hearing a pitched note at the same time in your head. Languages based on the fusion of image (pattern) and sound (frequency) would (to a musician) make a lot of sense.

Taking into account the simplicity of the apparatus required to set-up a cymatics system, this system of language development would have been highly possible. Quartz crystals are incredible resonators and are used in a number of acoustical ways in science and technology today. Egyptians began quarrying granite around 3000 B.C. and must have been extremely aware of its magical acoustic abilities. As John Reid points out, during the hollowing of the Sarcophagus, the resonation of the box and the harmonics being produced by the quartz crystals in the granite would have had an effect upon the stone masons, probably a therapeutic and aesthetic effect. It seems all too obvious to me that the granite used in the King's chamber would have been especially chosen for its acoustical and resonant properties in order to produce specific symbols of the Egyptian language. It still leads us back to this question: how did the designer of Rosslyn Chapel learn and apply the science of Cymatics in 1450 A.D.?

There is one very important clue to this and revolves around a man named Sir Gilbert Haye. Haye was born in Scotland and was one of the first students to receive a Masters degree at the fledgling St Andrews University in 1419. It is now believed by many historians that he was present in Roslin when building work started on the chapel in 1456. He was one of the "most learned and travelled men of his time," collecting rare scriptures and manuscripts to amass a vast library of knowledge which he eventually brought back to Rosslyn. He also mastered and spoke over sixteen languages fluently. He was tutor to the Anjou Family and had also met Joan of Arc during this time. He became tutor to Sir William Sinclair's children and confidant/advisor to the Earl Sinclair.

What is interesting to me is this: it is believed that Sir Gilbert Haye had travelled as far as Cathay (the old name for China) and if this is true, which I believe it is, then he would have travelled through India and Tibet to get there. Both of these areas of the world display an ancient knowledge of cymatics in their Sufi, Hindu, Vedic and Buddhist influences. In Tibet the famous Singing Bowls resemble flanged Chladni plates and serve a very similar purpose, using vibration and frequencies to direct the spiritual energies of the soul.

Yet, when we look at China and the 4000 years in the development of the art of Gong making, we really start to see how the influence of cymatics could have been understood and comprehended by an already extremely intellectual and inquisitive scholar. Gong making has been around in China since its earliest civilisation and is a highly developed and mystical art form. The tuning of gongs requires a highly skilled ear to pick up the wide range of harmonics produced which seem to pour out of the prolonged resonance of the gong in waves. A veritable symphony of harmonics! But in order to get the perfect tuning, sand is strewn across the flat surface of the gong and the pattern produced from the resonation will be a reflection of the frequency of the current state of the gong's pitch and harmonics.

Certainly there is a great deal of evidence to support the fact that the properties and potential of sound and vibration has been known and utilised within many eastern cultures for thousands of years. Perhaps we as a modern civilisation have over-looked this medium and by-passed it for more conventional needs, however it seems that ancient cultures and even religions have tapped in to this source of musical and scientific power and found ways of utilising it for the benefit of body, mind and soul. So it does not stretch the imagination too much to entertain the thought that knowledge of this science and its properties could have been understood and could have even been suppressed! Perhaps this knowledge went up in smoke along with The Library at Alexandria, who knows.

If Sir Gilbert Haye had soaked up the knowledge of any one of these eastern cultures, he most certainly would have returned to Rosslyn to integrate this knowledge of the effects of sound and vibration into the chapel stonework to be re-discovered in later generations: I have speculated already what the wonderment would have been in the reactions of Chladni, Margaret Watts Hughes or Dr Hans Jenny upon their discovery of the symbols in Rosslyn Chapel. It is like a time capsule of language awaiting sympathetic communication. The designer knew that "birds of a feather flock together" and one day in the future (and if Ernst Chladni had visited Rosslyn in 1790 it would only have been 250 years), someone would walk in and recognise the language and make a translation of the symbols for all to understand. But then again, a scientist could not discern the artistic and aesthetic realisation of the melodies produced from the translation. That has to be crafted by a musician and arranger for the music to be performed authentically. But then you could say Cymatics is the visual representation of music in nature and that a musician is already aware of these effects in their experience of being surrounded by melodic sound vibrations almost constantly and observing the effect upon an audience or individuals during acoustic performances.

I believe that the designer had every intention that it would be a musician who realised the music in the symbols, since the symbols are produced by the effect of sustained musical tones. Every serious musician at some stage in their development takes time to study the acoustical properties of the sounds they are producing from their instruments.

I have found that the entire subject and phenomenon of Cymatics has a great deal to do with The Platonic Solids and the physical building blocks of our universe. Imagine invisible form with the effect of invisible sound and observing it become visible. That concept is the subject of another intriguing book...

Fig. 10 : The divine proportions of sacred geometry built into the Grecian Temple have remained one of Man's finest and most artistic achievements throughout history. It was truly 'Music in Stone!'

Chapter 7
WYSIWYG -What you see is what you get
Translating the symbols into music

For a composer, it is a moment of inspiration, the spontaneous flash of creative thought that drives the ideas behind your music. Everything you have learned about in music, including technique, style, form and structure, up to that moment is merged into the fusion of your creation. You carry on until you are completely satisfied that you have created a unique and artistic composition encapsulating the spontaneous flash of creative thought that drove you to do it. Then you can appreciate it thereafter, as you have set it down in formal notation and as long as there are musicians who can read your music notation system.

On this occasion however, the music has already been composed, and the moment of inspiration has taken place many years ago. The creator has captured that creative inspiration in a notational form, and the creative task on my part is to understand this notational form and translate it into music using a formula. This formula will be a combination of musical academia and instinct; the search for cadences, Cymatics symbolism and their associated pitches, a good knowledge of Pythagorean tuning and Renaissance instruments.

We begin at The Apprentice Pillar (this is the direction of the music in my opinion, moving from South to North) and the first observation is the first two arches having similar opening notes. Is this a cadence or an opening motif? As I continue matching the cymatic symbols, a definite 'key' is beginning to emerge; **A minor**, the **aeolian mode**. This mode formed part of the music theory of ancient Greece, and is based around the relative natural scale of A , in a similar manner to playing all the 'white notes' of a piano from A to A. Greek theory called this simple scale the hypodorian mode, and the aeolian and locrian modes must have formed different (perhaps chromatic) variations of this form. The term 'aeolian mode' fell into disuse in mediaeval Europe, as church music based itself around eight musical modes: the relative natural scales in D, E, F and G, each with their authentic and plagal counterparts.

As I progressed, my attempts at pitch assignment and experiments with sections of cadences, I was finally bringing forth to my ear a melodic structure and phrasing. The sound of real music was gradually emerging, as a Polaroid photograph develops gradually before you. It was such a simple and haunting melody, very old and very like a nursery rhyme. This simple phrase is repeated again on the next arch only this time moving harmonically to the dominant major key. This harmonic progression is very indicative of Scandinavian folk music, where you move, for example, from the key of A minor into E major. Considering William St. Clair's connections with Orkney, this may not come as too much of a surprise.

Once I had finally covered every arch and its cubes, I could play back the melodies and begin to define their rhythmic measure. The most common combination of cubes on the arch sections are: nine to begin, then we reach an arch meeting point; then eight more cubes until the arch merges into the East wall. The melodic phrases have a definite feel of triple time in their structure and although there is great beauty that comes forth in duple time, the music is best suited (to my ears and logic) to 6/8 time and this falls perfectly and rhythmically into place at the end of each arch cadence. It was common practice in the fifteenth century to move without any warning from triple time to duple time and back again. This musical device I have adopted into the music score as I have read the cubes appearing on each arch as a "what you see is what you get". Or in musical terms "what you *feel* is what you *know*."

Placing the music into measurable format, I realised I had over 45 bars of musical themes and phrases that flowed and moved melodically and harmonically. How do we present this music with accompanying harmonies and chord structures?

Sourcing information about musical accompaniment in Scotland during the 15th century is very difficult, as there are very few documents around that give a detailed explanation in score form. A great deal of music has been lost over time and the few manuscripts that survive do not tell us a great deal. We have to turn to composers who were in fashion at the time such as John Dunstable, Guillaume Dufay and the Burgundian/Flemish Schools during the Renaissance. The Burgundian School was the first phase of activity of the Franco-Flemish School, the central musical practice of the Renaissance in Europe. Of all the names associated with the Burgundian School, the most famous was Guillaume Dufay, who was probably the most famous composer in Europe in the 15th century. He wrote music in many of the forms which were then current; music which was melodic, singable and memorable (more than half of his sacred music consists of simple harmonisations of plainsong, for example). They give us many clues regarding the common harmonic accompaniment of the time.

I am certain that the choice of instruments in the 'orchestra of angels' were specially chosen for their ability to accompany voices and perform popular dance/folk tunes such as they did at social gatherings and festivities. Fortunately, I had spent a great deal of my musical studies (over twenty years) researching and listening to medieval music and harmony. I had already acquired a good knowledge of what the tonal colour, rhythmic and harmonic qualities of the music of the 1400s contained. I knew there had to be some reason for having studied this period of music and now I could use this learning to my advantage and create an authentic realisation of the designer's intended music.

I have since applied the rhythms and harmonies to the Motet with all the instruments and voices into five distinct movements, while the Motet form usually denotes an unaccompanied vocal text. Another highly interesting part of my research was the *Inchcolm Antiphoner*, a music manuscript inscribed by monks on an island in the Firth of Forth, near Edinburgh dated at around 1300. Some of its Latin chants (in praise of St Columba) incorporate both music and texts that are believed to be of considerably greater ancient origin. Recent analysis of the latter manuscript – of which much remains to be done – provides strong evidence for a type of Celtic plainchant, representing a distinct regional evolution from the main European forms of this unaccompanied liturgical song. One aspect of this distinctiveness, in fact, may well have been that Celtic plainchant was accompanied, on an early version of the clarsach, or small Scottish harp. The organ was also established in Scotland by the 12th century.

It began to dawn on me that there could be a text for this music and an investigation must be made into what this could be. My findings were extremely interesting.

Chapter 8
An Orchestra of Angels -
The Carved Musicians

The question I am asked most frequently regarding the mystery of the cubes is this: "*what makes you believe it is music that the designer has concealed in symbolism?*"

The first time you walk into the Lady Chapel (at the east end of Rosslyn Chapel) you are immediately struck by the complexity and geometric beauty of the arches. As your eyes follow the arches to their meeting point on the pillars, the next objects that catch your eye will be the musicians performing upon their instruments, all along the length of the entire sequence of arches. The whole end of this chapel just emanates music, it is a symphony of geometric carvings and symbols complete with orchestra and choir.

The actual line up of musicians is highly indicative of a 15th century orchestra/band for soirées and musical evenings spent in the company of rich friends and acquaintances. Since an orchestra of this size would be a rather expensive affair, it clearly shows William St. Clair to be a musical man who could afford nothing but the best musicians and on a very grand scale.

Beginning with the agreed starting point of the piece, The Apprentice Pillar, we take note of the first musician in the line up, the Lute or Ud Player. He is wearing a turban, giving the impression that this is an individual from the East, Egypt or Arabia, or that this is simply a clue to the type of instrument he is playing. Whatever the reason for the headwear, it signifies the individuality of all of the musicians; no two look alike and they all possess a unique build and character as he is the first of three lutars (lutenists) in the orchestration. The carvings tell us a great deal about the instrument, and what looks very like (from its shape and size) a small four-course lute and in closer examination is to be plucked with a plectrum. All lutars are performing on similar instruments. This detail also gave us a good idea of what note range and musical function the instrument plays amongst the tonal colour of the piece.

The next musician to observe is what we believed to be a Psaltery or a type of medieval box lyre with five strings but as we have seen, under scrutiny this musical angel proved to be a 'decoy' with a very special message from the designer.

Next, there is a Fife and Tabor (see *fig. 11*). This combination of instruments was very popular for dances and outdoor festive occasions and often, these minstrels could juggle, mime and display a great variety of entertainment skills. This particular carving shows such detail that you can explicitly make out the 'bells' strapped to his wrists. A veritable 'One Man Band'. The earliest surviving manuscript of dance music is called *The Gresley Manuscript*, compiled in around 1500. It covers this instrument's role and appears to be full of tunes reminiscent of Italian 15th century dance music in which this instrument would certainly have played a part.. This could mean that the notation set out for this instrument by the designer of Rosslyn is of an even earlier reference than *The Gresley Manuscript*, by around 70 years.

We move onto the next arch in the sequence where we find the first of two figures who appear to be holding an open book, as if there is a text to be sung or spoken, yet there are definite pitches to be achieved from the line of cubes in their parts, with which this angel brings the Apprentice Pillar music to a close. We conclude that this is a solo singer or suggesting a small choir. (see *figs. 11 & 15*)

A shawm (see *fig. 12*) heralds the opening of The Journeyman's Pillar movement. This instrument has been mistaken for a trumpet in the past by many observers, but as you can see, his fingers are covering up to possibly five or six holes. This would have been impossible for a trumpet, as valves had not yet been developed at this time for brass instruments. These instruments were imported into Europe from Africa and the near East throughout the medieval period. They can have a powerful piercing sound and would be best employed outdoors or on ceremonial occasions. By the 15th century, the shawm, like many other instruments, had developed into a family of instruments.

Fig. 11: Fife and Tabor (left) and an 'angel' with the open book (right)
Notice the bells strapped to the wrist of the fife player.

Fig.12 : The Shawm

Like the crumhorn, the shawm had a double reed. In the case of the crumhorn, the reeds are protected inside a wooden chamber, but shawm players place the reeds inside their mouth with their lips against the bottom end of the reed, which allows the reed to vibrate freely.

Next comes a very easy to explain Tabor/Drum (*fig.11*) and his notation/cube sequence was one the easiest to understand, since the percussion notes do not vary in pitch and neither do the sequence of cubes as they are all the same line of one repetitive symbol.

The Organetto or 'Portative Organ' (*fig. 13*) is the central angel on this pillar. It is a very easy instrument to identify, although if you have never seen an organetto you would probably be at a loss to identify on what instrument the musician is performing. When you compare images of a performer on the organetto and the carving itself, it really is an exquisite piece of artistic description since this instrument is quite complex in appearance. It is basically a portable hand-bellowed pipe organ that could be played and carried at the same time. Composer Francesco Landini (c.1325/35-1397) was a virtuoso on the portative organ and wrote many compositions and poems incorporating the organetto as an accompaniment and solo instrument. The instrument fell into disuse by the middle of the 15th century.

To complete this Pillar, and toward the North end of the Lady Chapel, there is a fiddle, and a return of the shawm. We can then move to the most interesting Celtic element of the piece.

The Master Mason's Pillar begins with a recurring short phrase from the choir and swiftly moves into a 'lament' played on the Lowland Bagpipes. This is interesting in that the melodic line for the bagpipes fits in perfectly and could not have been composed for a better instrument to perform it. It almost seems written for this instrument. The colouristic flavour of these particular pipes, its sweetness of tone and amplitude bring a welcome Celtic influence to the work.

Fig. 13 : Illustration (left): Detail from 'Mary in the Rose Bower' by Hans Memling (1480-1510) (right): the Rosslyn organetto player

The next instrument is in our opinion is a shawm again, it has the same build as the previous instrument and being held in exactly the same manner.

Finally, a return to the lute draws the instrumental parts of the work to a close. The orchestra and singers are now identified and the instruments and players can now be brought together to perform the work.

I have put all my efforts into realising the true variety of sound and tonal colours that were first envisioned by the original designer/composer. Although most of these instruments lacked the technological means to encompass a wide note range, their limitations imparted the unique character to the instruments and therefore the colour and texture of the music. Listening to the instruments takes one back in time, as they create their medieval atmosphere of unique musical tone qualities and yet they can sound modern in many ways.

So to reiterate: *What makes us believe it is music that the designer has concealed in symbolism?*

.

Certainly the designer has gone to great lengths to show the detail of the performance techniques and capabilities of the instruments and performers. Nothing has been left to chance or guess work (except for the 'decoy' angel I discussed earlier). Therefore, it is my opinion that the carved musicians and the symbolic system of cubes which end in cadences at the end of each arch, would strongly signify to me that this is music, intended to be performed and sung once the symbols have been transposed into pitches by use of a formula and I believe that this is beyond any shadow of a doubt.

Before I leave the subject of the science of cymatics and the symbolism contained therein, I offer another example from the Chartres Cathedral in France, which has many similar features and carvings to Rosslyn Chapel. The three top photographs shown in *Fig. 14* are of the Chartres Labyrinth, and when enhanced graphically they show the cymatics symbol for the note F# which appears on the cymatics plate when the note is sounded by a native American flute. This is a further example of the science of cymatics embedded within the sacred geometry of the Gothic Cathedrals, and it is too coincidental not to be taken seriously.

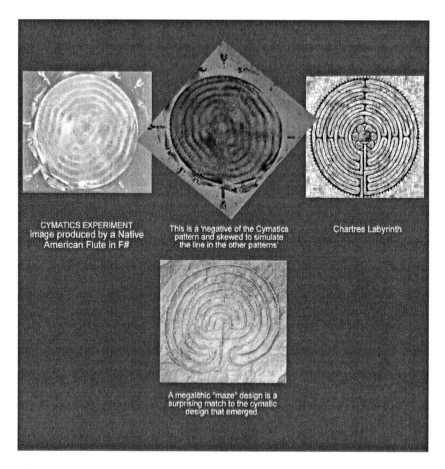

Fig. 14: The design of the Chartres Labyrinth and its relation to megalithic art and cymatics.

Chapter 9
The Resonance of *Ut Queant Laxis*

With such beautiful melodies and interesting melodic progressions in place, the structure and direction of the work was beginning to take form. Harmonic journeys through keys that best suited the instrument, the repeated 'melisma' that appeared (sometimes in reverse) and resolutions of cadences made the work's form appear like a great choral work.

There are two angels singing from an open book (*figs. 11 & 15*), perhaps suggesting that a text is to be used. This is one of the most obvious to the eye and also one of the most mysterious statements of any of the carvings in the Lady Chapel at Rosslyn. Firstly, we have to ask, what book is it he is holding. As the pages appear blank and give us no information regarding its contents, we are left to draw the assumption that the designer's metaphor is probably indicating the Holy Bible.

Fig. 15: Does this figure indicate that a text is set to the music?

On searching for a reference to any literary text in the chapel you find absolutely nothing but an inscription (pertaining to the Temple of Solomon); *'"Wine is strong, a King is stronger, Women are even stronger, but Truth conquers all"*

This is an interesting text with much background and legend attached to it but I felt it did not relate a great deal to the music; however, I took from it some interesting clues that pointed me in a different direction.

I then asked myself, *if* this music had been concealed, perhaps the music could have been an offence to the Church who (it is believed) banned the use of the interval of the augmented fourth from all secular music and hymns (its interval encompasses three whole tones or 'tritone'), because they felt that the 'dissonance' of the interval was a distraction to the worshippers, who were required to concentrate on the biblical text and not the music.

Medieval musicians also dubbed the tritone "The Diabolus in Musica" or the "Devil's Interval". (The Kyrie from Palestrina's *Missa Papae Marcelli* was printed in his Second Book of Masses. The work is famous, as it was said to have been composed to convince Pope Marcellus II not to ban polyphonic music from the liturgy. It is known fact that the esoteric school of Pythagoras taught that certain sounds can trigger several different states of mind. In later centuries, the church became aware of this and attempted to make illegal all the sounds and intervals that could bring sexual, joyful, sensual or other feelings. A great deal of Gregorian Chants abound with Augmented Fourths and tritones.

Throughout the Rosslyn Motet, the music sounds an Augmented fourth interval on four occasions and many times the melody jumps a tritone to great effect. Although this interval can appear dissonant, if it is 'prepared' harmonically it can produce the most beautiful and haunting sound to a melody. One of the greatest examples of using the tritone would be the first two notes of Leonard Bernstein's "Maria" from *West Side Story*; a more dramatic effect is produced in the "Mars" theme from Holst's *Planets Suite* where he prepares the ear for the tritone by jumping a fifth and lowering a semi-tone to create a tritone with a sinister tension. Conversely, *The Simpsons* cartoon theme uses the augmented fourth in a highly comical and entertaining way, so what we have here is a highly adaptable and effective musical phenomenon.

It becomes easy to understand why some people would choose to keep the effect of these sounds under control in the same way they practiced control over developments in architecture, astronomy, science, physics, art, literature, medicine and politics.

I began to look into hymns with any possible connection with the carvings in Rosslyn. One of the hymns I researched was *Ut Queant Laxis*, (written c. 800), which had great prominence since it related to the foundations of western musical notation, which as I have mentioned was invented by Guido de Arezzo, a monk of the Order of St. Benedict, who resided near Paris. He died at Avellano, near Arezzo in 1050. As I mentioned previously, he is most famous for inventing the system of staff-notation that is still in use, and rendered various other services to the progress of musical art and science.

Early in his career Guido could see that the music of the liturgy was being mis-read and variations on the original themes were being developed because the old neumes notational system was neither clear nor specific enough to be easily memorised and learned. Many of the singers and performers were improvising the melodies and distorting the themes. What Guido did was very ingenious - he used the first syllables of every verse of the Hymn to St John the Baptist and assigned them as singing syllables for each of the tones within the hexachord of the diatonic scale, creating a clear mnemonic:

Ut queant laxis	That [ut] your servants	UT (do)
Resonare fibris	May freely sing [resonare]	RE
Mira gestorum	The miracles	MI
Famuli tuorum	Of your deeds	FA
Solve poluti	Remove [solve] all stains	SOL
Labii reatum,	From their unclean lips [Labii],	LA
Sancte Ioannes!	"Saint John!"	SI

I looked into the source of the text of *Ut Queant Laxis* and found that the text is taken from Bible verses in Matthew 2:3 and tells of John the Baptist's time spent in the desert. This made a strong connection with the chapel because it is dedicated to St Matthew the Apostle, carrying on the tradition from the first chapel that was built on these grounds and that this hymn is a 'foundation stone' to western music notation makes perfect sense to me when we are being presented with a completely natural and new type of resonant notation in the form of cymatics.

Interestingly, there are thirteen stanzas to the hymn and also thirteen melodic arches emanating from the pillars which is possibly why the text matched up so well in form and meaning. Everything seemed to fit perfectly, the text carried the melodies beautifully and it became very easy to set the text into the form and structure of the music.

There was a sense of inevitability about the sound of the work now with the Hymn to St John. (If there is a possible connection between the designer of the chapel and The Knights Templar, then this hymn would carry even more weight, knowing that this mysterious order were also known as The Knights of St John or alternatively 'The Johnites'.

The full text of the Hymn follows.

Ut queant laxis resonare fibris
O Mira gestorum famuli tuorum,
Solve polluti labii reatum,
Sancte Joannes.

O for thy spirit, holy John, to chasten
Lips sin-polluted, fettered tongues to
loosen; So by thy children mighty thy
deeds of wonder Meetly be chanted.

Nuntius celso veniens Olympo,
Te patri magnum fore nasciturum,
Nomen, et vitæ seriem gerendæ
Ordine promit.

Lo, a swift herald, from the skies
descending,
Bears to thy father promise of thy
greatness; How he shall name thee,
what thy future story, Duly revealing.

Ille promissi dubius superni,
Perdidit promptæ modulos loquelæ;
Sed reformasti genitus peremptæ
Organa vocis.

Scarcely believing message so
transcendent, Him for a season power
of speech forsaketh, Till, at thy birth-
time, once again returneth, Voice to
the voiceless.

Ventris obstruso recubans cubili
Senseras Regem thalamo manentem;
Hinc parens nati meritis uterque
Abdita pandit.

Thou in thy mother's womb all darkly
cradled, Knewest thy Monarch, biding
in His chamber, Whence the two
parents, through their children's
merits Mysteries uttered.

Sit decus Patri, genitæque Proli,
Et tibi, compar utriusque virtus,
Spiritus semper, Deus unus omni
Temporis ævo. Amen.

Praise to the Father, to the Son
begotten, And to the Spirit, equal
power possessing, One God whose
glory, though the lapse of ages, Ever
resoundeth. Amen

Antra deserti teneris sub annis,
Civium turmas fugiens, petisti,
Ne levi posses maculare vitam
Crimine linguæ.

Thou, in thy childhood, to the desert
caverns. Fleddest for refuge from the
cities' turmoil, Where the world's
slander might not dim thy lustre,
Lonely abiding.

Præbuit durum tegumen camelus
Artubus sacris, strophium bidentes;
Cui latex haustum, sociata pastum
Mella locustis.

Camel's hair raiment clothed thy
saintly members, Leathern the girdle
which thy loins encircled ; Locusts
and honey, with the fountain-water,
Daily sustained thee.

Ceteri tantum cecinere Vatum
Corde præsago jubar affuturum;
Tu quidem mundi scelus auferentem
Indice prodis.

Oft in past ages, seers with hearts
expectant Sang the far-distant advent
of the Day-Star; Thine was the glory,
as the world's Redeemer First to
proclaim him.

Non fuit vasti spatium per orbis Sanctior quisquam genitus Joanne, Qui nefas sæcli meruit lavantem Tingere lymphis.	Far as the wide world reacheth, born of woman, Holier was there none than John the Baptist Meetly in water laving Him who cleanseth Man from pollution.
Sit decus Patri, genitæque Proli, Et tibi, compar utriusque virtus, Spiritus semper, Deus unus omni Temporis ævo. Amen.	Praise to the Father, to the Son begotten, And to the Spirit, equal power possessing, One God whose glory, though the lapse of ages, Ever resoundeth. Amen.
O nimis felix, meritique celsi, O Nesciens labem nivei pudoris, Præpotens Martyr, nemorumque cultor, Maxime Vatum.	More than blessed, merit high attaining, Pure as the snow-drift, knowing no defilement, Mightiest martyr, dweller in the desert, Greatest of prophets.
Serta ter denis alios coronant Aucta crementis, duplicata quosdam, Trina te fructu cumulata centum Nexibus ornant.	Thirty-fold increase some with glory crowneth; Sixtyfold fruitage prize for others winneth; Hundredfold measure, thrice repeated, decks thee Blest one, for guerdon.
Nunc potens nostri meritis opimis O Pectoris duros lapides revelle Asperum planans iter, et reflexos Dirige calles.	May the virtue of thine intercession, All stony hardness from our hearts expelling, Smooth the rough places, and the crooked straighten, Here in the desert.
Ut pius mundi Sator et Redemptor Mentibus culpæ sine labe puris Rite dignetur veniens beatos Ponere gressus.	Thus may our gracious Maker and Redeemer, Seeking a station for his hallowed footsteps, Find, when he cometh, temples undefiled Meet to receive him.
Laudibus cives celebrent superni Te, Deus simplex pariterque trine, Supplices et nos veniam precamur: Parce redemptis. Amen.	Now, as the Angels celebrate thy praises, God everlasting, Trinity, Co-equal, Spare thy redeemed ones, as they bow before thee, Pardon imploring. Amen

Chapter 10
The Cosmic Scale

As the Lady Chapel gave up its secrets and the music emerged from the carvings, I began to realise that I could not take the Lady Chapel out of context with the rest of the Chapel and simply treat the carvings between the pillars in isolation. The totality of the carvings and their message has to be read, with the Lady Chapel as the focal point of the total message. Much of the symbology within the carvings points to nature, as for instance in the number of representations of the Green Man.

It is blatantly obvious to me at this point that the music concealed in the arches between the pillars is the focal point for all that is going on in the Chapel and it is the music that pulls all of the threads together into one glorious message. I was reminded of the scientific concept of the creation of the universe when it was summed up as the 'Big Bang'. Here we have a scientific representation of a Divine event sounding the first note of the Cosmic Scale.

I have proved to my own satisfaction that the cymatic patterns derived from musical notes have a common thread to all created objects. Each object has its own unique resonant frequency vibration just as musical notes have their harmonic resonant frequency. Rosslyn Chapel's cubes are a demonstration of how to use cymatics to formulate musical notation. The musical scale is in fact a perfect mirror in which to view the processes of creation, beginning with the first note of the Big Bang all the way to the incredible variety of the biosphere on earth. Cymatics also reflects the laws of sound upon nature.

A resonant frequency vibration sets up an invisible pattern which can be either sound or electrical, and which is taken up by particles of matter, thus making the invisible pattern visible as a physical object. Each pattern is unique, just as a thumbprint is a unique way of identifying an individual. One can experience music as divine shapes allied to the unique resonant harmonic frequencies of each note, and in so doing you can also be aware of listening to the Divine mechanics of Creation. Recent research in quantum physics tells us that, the nature of matter is underpinned by one vast quantum field - the Zero Point Field, an ocean of microscopic vibrations in the space between things. This tells us that at a subatomic level, everything is connected to everything else like an invisible web. It also tells us that we are all connected to one another and to everything else in this universe to a far greater extent than we ever imagined. I also realised that in our daily exchanges with others, we are all performing a cymatic series of patterns with the cadence of our voices, which is unique to each individual and is instantly recognisable. It served to remind me that all of us in our own unique way are demonstrating the basic shapes and rhythms of life and taking part in the great symphony, which began with the Big Bang.

I had to go down the road of pre-history to find out that we had forgotten more than we know and many basics truths have vanished into the mists of time in one sense, but remain before us in another. Quantum physics is now showing us the way back.

The gift of Rosslyn Chapel tells us that the Holy Grail is a metaphor for the Truth and the Truth is written all around in the carvings and the divine proportions of the Chapel for all with eyes to see. The gift is, for those who see this Truth, that each and every one of us are connected, whether we know it or not, by the music of the great Cosmic Scale of Creation. By seeing our connection to the Divine Harmonics of the universe, we can awaken spiritually to become aware of the Divine Harmonies being played out around us and, by so doing, we connect once more to our heritage as a part of the Divine whole. What greater message could have been left to posterity than this? What better way to express the Holy Grail than this message of harmony carved into the ceiling and the arches of the Chapel?

As above – so below.

Chapter 11
The Law of Resonance and its Relationship to Sound

Whilst studying music and in particular the qualities and ratios of the diatonic scale, I became aware of the Law of Resonance. This is a subject that seems to have been side-lined to a degree and yet it is one of the most basic laws in physics from the point of view that it connects all things and keeps everything orderly. The *resonant frequency* of any object is its unique 'thumbprint' which separates it from other objects and it is the rate at which that object vibrates. It is this law that makes music possible, to produce individual notes and their harmonic relationships with the other notes in the scale.

I realised that the following definition can be applied to the science of cymatics that I used to find the actual notes and their unique pitch, using the symbols carved into the ceiling of the arches in the Chapel. Each symbolic design is representative of a particular pitch or note in the ancient diatonic musical scale and each vibrates at its own unique resonant frequency. The science of cymatics, and how it was used, was fully explained in detail in Chapter 6.

Here is the definition of the term 'resonant frequency', which will help in understanding the way I have applied it.

Resonant Frequency: The condition where two bodies or systems have the same sympathetic vibration, one to the other. Size is not relevant, only the resonant frequency. A good example of this would be two tuning forks of different size, but both tuned to vibrate at middle C. If one were struck in the proximity of the other then the other fork would sound in sympathy, with the same 'resonant vibration'.

Without this law creating order and relationships, the whole of creation would descend into chaos. The law of resonance is omni-present throughout creation and extends from the spiritual to the temporal bringing order and harmony. It is easy to see why music is the basic 'mirror' of creative relationships in the physical reality.

One can see this law at work in the science of cymatics. Each symbol and its shape is in fact a resonant frequency representation of the particular note, frozen in stone. When a note is vibrating at it own 'thumbprint' frequency, it produces a 'print' of its identity which can be produced and 'recorded' by carving the symbolic shape of its print in the stone cubes. Thus we can say at this point that in one sense the carved symbols are the symbolic recordings of the notes of the motet arranged in sequence in the arches.

Here is a definition of the words used in the statement.

Resonance is the state of a system or body in which a large vibration is produced by a small stimulus of approximately the same frequency as that of the system.

To resonate is to vibrate in sympathy.

Sympathy is the condition where a thing responds to the action of another with affinity or correlation.   .

Frequency is the number of vibrations in a unit of time.

Vibration is oscillation—to change to and fro rapidly.

Resonant Frequency is the condition where two bodies or systems have the same sympathetic vibration one to the other. In this instance, size is not relevant, only the resonant frequency.

Amplitude: Extent, scope, magnitude.

Induction: The process by which electrical or magnetic properties are transferred, without physical contact, from one circuit or body to another (as in any normal electrical transformer)

The above law works in exactly the same manner for either electrical phenomena or sound. It is inherent throughout the entire universe and is part of the operation of the super spectrum. The physical universe is based on energy and these energies form a super spectrum from the basest physical objects to the finest aesthetic wavelengths. Each layer of the spectrum has its own resonant 'thumbprint' or wavelength, which is synonymous with its own particular resonant frequency.

A resonant frequency can be understood by using two tuning forks as an example. The size of each tuning fork is not relevant, only the frequency at which it is vibrating. If one fork is struck in the proximity of the other, then the fork at rest will begin to vibrate in sympathy at the same frequency as the other. In other words, one fork duplicates the vibrations of the other.

The Rosslyn Vortex

From my own researches, I have ascertained that the 'Rosslyn Vortex', or place of power, is sited in the original lower Chapel directly behind the position of the arches between the pillars. These vortices are often associated with blind springs or water near the sacred sites. Rosslyn chapel may have a resonant code carved into the body of the chapel, which probably contains the key to the incantation, or resonant frequency in the form of a musical phrase that 'opens' the vortex to the consciousness of the Spiritual Being and thus the Holy Grail of spiritual progress can be achieved. Could it be that this 'musical phrase' is contained in the music of the cubes?

Chapter 12
The Diatonic Scale -
The First Principle of Reality

Taking as our starting point the statement, "In the beginning was the word and the word was with God", we see in this that through the mist of mistranslation and alteration, the original Cause was sounding the diatonic doh (*ut* in the medieval terminology). It becomes the first particle and then breaks down into its ratios of harmonics and partials, forming the elements of physical reality. The musical diatonic scale is a reflection in sound of this first scale just as the rainbow is a reflection in light and colour of the same principle, which governs all of the actions and reactions of physical reality.

Because all arises from that first particle (what science calls the Big Bang), then everything throughout the universe is related and connected by the principle of the diatonic scale and its harmonics. It is the key to connecting with the universe at large and its principles, through the law of resonance. Everything has its own individual resonant frequency, yet the fundamental principle and the law of diatonic harmony is the same for all. Just as in music, it is the same harmony and chords in a different key at a different pitch. To resonate with something you merely have to find its resonant frequency to connect with it. Size is irrelevant.

Where science may have a 'missing link' is in its understanding of physics and the physical reality in the area of Cause. It is the point where physical science crosses over into the spiritual and recognises the element of Cause in its equation. Cause has the same effect in analogy as a catalyst. It has to be present to initiate and speed up a chemical reaction, yet of itself it is neither changed nor affected by the reaction.

One humorous way of understanding the presence of Cause in reality is to consider the game of *Monopoly*. Without the involvement of a number of 'cause points' (players), it is just a heap of meaningless cardboard.

These cause points operate through a physical reality terminal, i.e. a body, which merely reflects the intentions of the invisible cause point just as the particles and diatonic scale principles of physical reality reflect the intentions of the original Cause. Keeping this in mind, the cause factor becomes blatantly apparent within physical reality and the business of life and livingness as the cause is reflected at all times through music, art, harmony, nature, colour, form, and design. Love, beauty and the universe at large reveal themselves as one great diatonic harmony.

This can be summed up in an axiom that says, "There are only two states to be considered: that which Creates, and that which is Created. From this original condition, all other conditions arise".

Chapter 13
Historical Threads

To fully understand the background to Rosslyn Chapel, we have to be aware of the great number of threads that make up a colourful tapestry of history going back thousands of years. Much has been written about the history of the Knights Templar and their historic connections with Rosslyn and the Freemasonry movement, but the esoteric history goes back much further in time.

The site on which the Chapel sits belongs to a period in prehistory when a now-vanished civilisation ruled the then-known world. It was this group of people who founded the Sumerian civilisation of Mesopotamia around 3000 B.C., in the present country of Iraq. We know a great deal about this early civilisation as they were diligent record keepers, and a huge number of stone tablets have been excavated over the years, outlining every facet of their daily lives. Most of these tablets are scattered around the universities and museums of Europe and the Americas, but enough material has been gleaned for us to realise that the Sumerians bequeathed, to the world, the basis for our present day civilisations.

What is not so well known is that the founders of the Sumerian civilisation are well documented in their tablets as the "gods who walked amongst men". The tablets and cylinders refer to them as the *Anunnaki*, or "they who from heaven came", and they are also referred to in Genesis in the Old Testament as the *Nefilim*. This part of early history has never been properly scientifically researched, and remains on the perimeter of the 'respectable' history books and historical paradigms, simply because the data and the information on the tablets is too controversial or unacceptable to academic authorities.

This situation originated in the 19th century when excavations first began and science had not advanced far enough, nor would religion allow the society at that time to understand the amazing claims being made on the tablets regarding the Sumerian 'gods' and their behaviour and achievements. In the usual time-honoured fashion, it was all swept under the academic carpet and assigned to the convenient bin labelled 'myths'.

Whatever the present day establishment view is, it is still to a great extent based on 19th century values, viewpoints and belief systems. If this were not the case, we would know much more about the early history of man and the story of civilisation from the hard evidence, even if it contradicts present day belief systems.

In following chapters, I go into much more detail regarding the 'contradictions' and point out the hard evidence that can still be seen around the planet to support the claim that a race of highly civilised Beings lived here on Earth and founded the first real civilisations.

To make the connection to Rosslyn Chapel and its abiding mystery, which maintains the interest and attention of successive generations, we have to begin with that early Sumerian civilisation and the so-called 'gods who walked amongst men'.

Let us look at the basic assumption that Rosslyn Chapel is the end point of a pilgrimage route from St James of Compostelo. The route visits seven points of power on which cathedrals have been built. These places of power, or node points, connect up earth lines, which are known as 'ley lines'. The energy lines represent the 'earth grid' of magnetic lines of energy around the Earth, which carry the energies being received from the sun and the cosmos, and those energies fluctuate with the changing seasons and sun cycles. At some time in the distant past, an advanced race identified, surveyed and laid out these lines on the surface of the earth for specific reasons, at which we can now only guess. That evidence points to the Anunnaki as the most likely builders of this system. In esoteric circles, some of this science and truth regarding the structure of earth energies has been passed down from antiquity and put to use on known earth grid routes.

The Rosslyn pilgrimage route is one of the surviving journeys that have been made for centuries by devout pilgrims. There has always been a belief, dating back to antiquity, that the energies contained at those places of power have a beneficial effect on the spirit of man. After all, man as part of the biosphere on earth represents the microcosmos within the macrocosmos of Earth, and he can share in the super spectrum of cosmic energies contained within the vortex on which the Holy places are built. This has been the belief in esoteric circles for millennia.

Take for instance the fairly recent research that has isolated positive ions in the air as being the problem which causes a 'sick building syndrome' where people who work in this environment become unwell. By enriching the air with an electronic negative ion fountain, the problem is solved. It proves that we are much more dependent on the electrical energies that surround us than we are aware. A good example of this that most people would recognise is the feeling of oppression before a thunderstorm followed by the relief and a feeling of well being directly after the storm. This inevitably raises the current question of electronic pollution caused by mobile telephones and other electronic devices that flood our environment with microwaves. Time will soon tell if this pollution is more dangerous than we suspect.

It is interesting that the musicians depicted on the top of the pillars in the Chapel, are playing medieval instruments. These very instruments were portable and were carried by pilgrims as described by Geoffrey Chaucer in his descriptive writings on the medieval pilgrimages to Canterbury in England. Music played a large part in the esoteric pilgrimages and it is no surprise that they turn up in the Chapel in a conspicuous place in the arches where the encoded music resides.

Music is spiritual food and is absolutely fundamental to the dimension of creation via its sacred mathematics, which when translated into sacred geometry gives us the sublime proportions of great buildings and music in stone which, when related mathematically to one or other of the sacred oracles, will resonate at that particular frequency. This spiritual resonation was the aim and purpose of the pilgrimage to those specific places where the human spirit could share in the sublime resonation of the perfect divine proportions of the buildings, which were designed to resonate and emulate them.

There is no doubt that the ancient race who laid out the ley system knew those very secrets of music and the divine proportions and designed and built a monumental system which spanned the Earth. They went to a very great deal of trouble to establish the ley system worldwide as a foundation for their spiritual, scientific and energy requirements. The system tapped into the Earth's unlimited free energy, across a large section of the super spectrum with the understanding that the physical and the cosmic energies were there to be harnessed for several purposes including energies from the biosphere, from the Earth's magnetic field and from the cosmos at large. How they implemented the energies and for what specific purposes can only be guessed at from the few, but monumental, structures that survived the cataclysmic effects of the Biblical flood.

All of this information is not pure speculation, but is based on hard evidence that has been around all along in the form of monumental structures such as the pyramids of Egypt and the South Americas. The massive stone platform of Baal-bek, in Lebanon, is reputed to be a former enclave of the Anunnaki and the worldwide ley system. All of these structures were massive enough to survive the flood and they remain to this day as recognisably the handiwork of an advanced race of engineers, and it is also evident that even with our present technology we would find it difficult to emulate them. For this and other reasons, I find it difficult to understand why the present archaeological and scientific establishments cannot or will not give this evidence and this critical area of our history the attention it deserves.

Chapter 14
The Comma of Pythagoras

I have slotted in the final missing piece to my study of the sacred geometry of creation and its mathematical relationship to music, with special reference to the basic diatonic scale. To achieve the full picture, I joined up all of the dots going back to my study of the mathematics of the diatonic scale with the emphasis on the tuning of the scale to compensate for the discrepancy known as the 'comma of Pythagoras' and for which the system of 'equal temperament' was devised, and which was much loved by J.S. Bach, who wrote a suite of music to demonstrate it, known as *The Well Tempered Clavier*. For many years, I could not find the reason why there was this harmonic discrepancy that caused a small fault in the perfect maths of the scale to double each time it was raised by an octave. In fact, if a piano tuner did not 'temper' the scale at middle C, by the time he had gone up by four octaves, the piano was totally out of tune to the ear of a musician.

Then I discovered that there is a term in physics called the 'uncertainty principle' (discovered by Heisenberg), which fits with the mathematics of the diatonic scale. This uncertainty principle exists in physical reality and also in music as the 'comma of Pythagoras', which occurs between E/F and B/C, and in each case conforms to the decimal 1.0136. This tiny decimal is the random factor that allows creation to take place both in the universe and in music. For instance, hydrogen could not transmute to helium without the comma of Pythagoras and creation would end right there.

Music is a mirror image of what takes place in the physical universe, but the 'perfect mathematics' of a mechanical universe leaves no 'space' for creation to enter and have an effect on the static mechanics of a lifeless mechanical system, thus the comma of Pythagoras creates that space and fulfils the role of Creator, by creating a 'crack in the universe' through which the Spiritual force of creation can enter and leave bringing the spiritual creative force into physical reality and giving it meaning and form.

This 'crack in the universe' is the space between the dimensions of the physical mechanical reality and the creative Spiritual Universe. It is here that the Spirit reaches and withdraws to the physical universe and as Eleazor the Essene said, "That which the spirit touches, grows and flourishes, and that which it abandons, withers and dies".

Finally, the last piece in the puzzle came when I connected information I had obtained—while a member of a Gurdjieff group—in the shape of a diagram called the Enneagram. This diagram shows the basic diatonic scale represented as a 'spiritual octave to the sun' but which retains the same aspects of the diatonic scale. Between the notes E/F and B/C, there are two mathematical semitones that do not 'fit' properly as the notes on either side are whole tones. Gurdjieff called this "The point of the first conscious shock where something can take place if a person is conscious".

I never really understood it until I read and understood the function of the comma of Pythagoras.

The early Egyptians called this science "the great secret of the Eye of Horus" within which was contained the mathematics of physics and the diatonic scale. It occurs to me that the diatonic scale is the spiritual representation of the creative aspect of the physical universe and is the reason that music is so fundamental to the life of the human race.

Chapter 15
Earth Energy and
Sacred Geometry of the Ancients

There is little or no difference between our understanding of electricity and that of the ancients except that our scientific establishments have not understood the resonant levels of earth energy and spiritual energy, which are only levels operating on the self-same laws but at higher and more aesthetic vibrations.

Sacred geometry has a great deal of involvement in this area as the cathedrals and places of power are focused by the structures built on them using the sacred geometrical shapes which attract and hold the energies just as an antenna attracts and holds radio and TV wavelengths to guide them to our sets: in other words, the pyramids are focusing antennas.

The 'Feathered Serpent' was the name for Thoth who was the ancient world scientist who taught mankind that the Serpent was the cosmic power which he tamed for use within the civilised world of that time.

Ours is a consumer society and much of the use of this power is flippant and ill understood, and there is an entire lost and ancient science of electronics based mainly on the earth energies and managed by the use of natural objects which are electrically sensitive—like quartz and granite—and the use of pyramid structures based on sacred geometry which focuses this cosmic power.

Where we miss out most of all is in the 'bridging' from the basic earth energies to the spiritual energies that are inherent and senior to the physical reality but nevertheless operating on the same laws.

Chapter 16
Ley Lines and Places of Power

Since the era of satellite observations of the earth's surface, we have discovered that the entirety of the land masses have at some time in antiquity been surveyed and set out with a pattern of lines and mounds like a huge grid or circuit board. There seems little doubt that this pattern of lines represents a massive scientific device, designed perhaps to utilize the magnetic field of the earth and its energies.

Whatever the reason, this vast network is still visible today after thousands of years of changes on the surface of the planet. It says a great deal about the skills of the civilisation that built it and their grasp of a technology that perhaps in some ways surpassed our own. The task of surveying and laying out this system worldwide today would strain even our technologies to the limit.

This is evidence on a grand scale that has the potential of turning history on its head if only the scientific community examined the evidence and took it on board. From other evidence recently presented it would appear that the great Biblical flood, or perhaps it may have been a shift in the position of the Earth's poles, swept away that entire civilisation but left us with the ruins of an enigmatic science. It makes one wonder at the power and knowledge of such a society and how different it was from our own.

Bits and pieces of this science have survived in esoteric or magical circles and, as for instance, the sites of Cathedrals and pilgrimage ways. The route to Rosslyn Chapel may be one of these routes, and a direct connection to a time on earth when a different science and a different set of values obtained.

It is also my considered opinion that the ley line earth grid, described above, is the 'nervous system' of the earth's biosphere, which is gathering the cosmic and sun energies from the great ocean of energy that surrounds the earth.

These energies are stored within each vortex at intersections within the grid and which is in constant flux as the

The places associated with the Dragon legend, are described as nerve centres of seasonal fertility & ancient sanctity.

Cathedrals, churches & holy places, including stone circles are all sited on ley lines. This tradition is lost in antiquity.

Dragons have positive & negative aspects as portrayed in fairy tales.It is analogous of electricity, which is useful only when harnessed, otherwise it can kill..

So called "Pagan religions" had their temples at particular points on the ley lines and always conducted their rites and practices at these points.

In myth and legend, ley lines are referred to as the "Dragon Path." Dragons breath fire (earth energy) The legends are a world wide phenomena and closely related to religion, as in the stories of the Saints who were dragon slayers.

St Michael & St George are sited as dragon slayers. Churches named after them abound and are to be found on the main ley lines which cross the country. One such line runs from St Michael's Mount to St Michael's Tor at Glastonbury

DRAGONS
"The Dragon Pulse"

RELIGION
SPIRITUAL/OCCULT

LEY LINES
"Old Straight Track"

U.F.O.'S

EARTH ENERGIES
ASTRONOMY

Silbury Hill, a man made structure looks exactly like a UFO when viewed from above. UFO's favour areas around ley lines and are often seen in what are known as "window areas" around stone circles and monuments.

In prehistoric time, a huge network of ley lines was laid down world wide like a vast circuit board, to store and control both earth & cosmic energies. This could only have been done by a civilization having the technology and mathematical skills to undertake such a vast project.

St Catherine is associated with the "fiery wheel" aerial phenomena. These dragons and fiery wheels are said to guard the treasure of the "Serpent Mounds or Barrows." This treasure is probably the secret of ley power or earth energy.

NASA has surveyed the earth and found the ley system to be worldwide. There had to be a technology in the past to move the massive blocks of quartz and granite to build the stone circles which were an integral part of the system.

AREAS OF LEY LINE RELATIONSHIPS
CROSS-REFERENCED

The lines and stone circles also had astronomical uses and were laid out with great accuracy to plot the solstices as an instance.

70

energies flow around the grid. These vortices have always been associated with 'places of power' and have been sites of pilgrimage for centuries. This is why they were used for ceremonies and initiations at special times where contact with the power of the grid was achieved by resonance brought about by special incantations or chanting. It could be used for good or evil provided the correct method was employed.

At this time, when there is a new pulse flooding the solar system as reported by NASA, these new and powerful energies are permeating every atom on the planet to bring about a shift in the evolution of the planet. The grid and the vortices around it, if contacted by the law of resonance, can connect the collective consciousness to these new and powerful vibrations and effect a connection to the higher level of esoteric powers of the energy. This was fully understood by the ancients who laid out the original ley system.

For many years, I have read book after book that outlines a different view of history and prehistory, simply by presenting evidence and artefacts that do not fit with the textbook theories. I have come to the conclusion that the Biblical flood was a reality and was one corner of a worldwide cataclysm that wiped out a previous civilization, and all we have of that civilization are a few vague memories and the ley system.

One school of thought says the axis of the earth changed from the near vertical to an inclination of 23 degrees. This happened around 10,000 years ago and tells us that history must be rewritten with this in mind. What we must do is to look at any previous sophisticated civilization from its own viewpoint and not from our own technological viewpoint, for a previous civilization would have taken an entirely different path than our own, and yet may have used forms of power of which we are still ignorant.

Perhaps it was more spiritually based and was more aware of the subtle energies of the earth, thereby building the ley system. The basic principles of the system seem to have been preserved to some extent in China and it is there we should begin our study. It would seem to me that they had a much broader view of our relationship to the universe at large and just how we as human beings fitted into it, how we as the microcosmos integrated with the macrocosmos.

Man seems to have lost his way in terms of his place in the greater scheme of things and somehow I feel that the ley system and the stone circles were man's way of remaining connected to the creative whole and the entire birth, life, death cycle.   This is why I feel it is an important study, for we are now becoming aware through science of the subtle energies which exist to hold the fabric of the physical universe together, but most of all that it comes down to the creative powers of the Spirit which gave birth to the physical universe. This seems to me to be the direction in which we are going, in this new century, for we must reconnect or perish.

Civilization and the Age of Man

One of the things that interests me greatly is the true age of civilization, as opposed to the accepted and very recent views on man and his origins. Much of this is based on 19th century concepts that, to a great degree, rejected the religious for the purely scientific. You cannot swing the pendulum through 180 degrees and totally reject one system for another, especially if the system you are rejecting has served mankind—however badly—for many years.

The truth always lies somewhere between the opposites and there is much historical detail which can be derived from Genesis in the Bible account of the Flood. Add to this archaeological evidence and scientific study and the resulting package will be nearer the truth. There is absolutely no doubt by the accumulated evidence that a pre-deluge civilization existed and instead of arguments about who is right in the religious and scientific viewpoints, much could be gained by co-operation between the various experts to ascertain just what shape it took. There are too many personal opinions and too many blind beliefs that muddy the waters of speculation.

Expert opinions could be pooled to piece together the prehistory of man by using all available resources, rather than one rejecting the other as nonsense. This could throw new light on the subject of the utilization of earth energies and possible prehistoric scientific civilizations.

Out of place Artefacts

As the years go on, the old 18th and 19th century dogmas about the origins of man and his civilizations become more and more tired and at the mercy of new scientific and archaeological techniques We find more and more artefacts which cast doubt upon the long-held dogmatic beliefs as to how man progressed from the caves to the cities. An 'Out of Place Artefact' is an item that turns up in the wrong time and place and contradicts the prevailing theories that have been taught from the orthodox textbooks for many years. They are usually swept swiftly under the carpet and ignored, or given misleading explanations. However, the pressure is growing to bring this out into the open and rewrite the textbooks. This comes back to the idea of a personal 'Reality Window', of which our ingrained beliefs define the dimensions.

We have to allow these things to go through our window and at least reassess them in light of new developments. Perhaps it would prevent us making the same mistakes the old civilisations made or, perhaps, prepare us to handle events on a world scale that recur from time to time.

Over the years, I have read many books that have touched on the idea of a vanished civilization in one way or another. It has been given many names, like Atlantis, Mu or Shangri La. There have been many more theories expounded on how it came to vanish and why, but these theories are merely opinions and sometimes obsessions which have to be taken with the proverbial pinch of salt. There is no doubt now in the minds of the serious researchers that, indeed, a civilization did pre-empt the Sumerian and Egyptian cultures and that it came to a sudden and violent end. What I have gleaned from these various books, and what I have deduced from my own ideas and perhaps hunches, is that it has much to do with a worldwide civilization that surveyed and laid down the ley system and which was operated from a central point.

Sometime before the flood, there was a pyramid culture which erected the step pyramids and the Egyptian pyramids for a particular reason, not just as burial chambers. They are too big and complex to have such a mundane explanation. I believe these pyramids to be part of the worldwide ley system and quite obviously the amount of time and labour put into the system was monumental and had to have a purpose of great, if not vital, importance to the survival of that civilization. The power gleaned from this huge network had physical and spiritual significance. It was obviously, as at Stonehenge, orientated as a celestial observatory, to plot the year and times of planting and harvesting, so that the most advantageous times for fertility could also be plotted.

The system must have used the magnetic flow lines of the biosphere and these were corrected and guided by the ley lines. Energy must have been stored in the stone circles and mounds, much as the condensers in a circuit board. In fact, a vast circuit board is a good analogy. Add to this that the pyramids, and certain monumental stones, drew cosmic energy from the atmosphere, and you have a picture of the circuit at work. This energy changed and was in constant flux throughout the year and across eleven-year sun cycles, and this had to be plotted and regulated to make the best use of the energy available. The energy we are talking about here can be seen in part in the displays of Aurora Borealis. There is also little doubt that the energy was used in some spiritual way, for it is interesting to note that practically all of the major centres of spiritual worship are sited on specific spots on these ley lines. There seems to be some sort of fine and creative energies available on these sites.

The evidence of recent surveys of the earth, from satellites, shows this vast network on every continent, so the evidence is there for all to see. It does not take much imagination to assess the task facing any organisation undertaking a worldwide task of such magnitude. Only in this century could it be said that we were in a position to try to emulate such a feat of engineering and I very much doubt if it could be done.

There must have been a central authority with worldwide access and the engineering skills to undertake such a huge task. This involved the same skills as motorway building but also involved cutting and moving huge stones of 200 tons or more, over hundreds of miles and then being placed accurately on site, on arrival. This was not the work of primitive men with stone or bronze tools—these men were engineers, surveyors, astronomers and highly cultured scientists. That their work has survived to the present day is a tribute to their workmanship and skill, and deserves better notice than is given.

They obviously had a very different science to our own and their culture must have developed very differently. Perhaps they had sources of knowledge and power that we are not yet aware, as for instance, we were not aware of radio or television before the latter part of the nineteenth century.

It is my feeling that their science was much more orientated to their mental and spiritual powers and what we now call magic or alchemy was the norm. To someone who has not seen a television set or used a computer, it would also seem like sheer magic, so we must not use the term 'magic' in the fairytale sense but in the technological sense. To the ignorant, technology *is* magic.

Something important and useful was lost then and all we are left with is the pale shadow of that magnificent civilisation in myth and legend.

Several commentators have remarked recently that since we are now well into the 21st century, then we can take a more positive attitude to what we do have in the way of evidence. These commentators cite Genesis in the Bible as a historical document that tells us what actually happened to that civilization, once we have removed it from the 19th century attitude of myth. There was a cataclysm, which in part was predicted and some sort of survival scenario was instituted whereby something of the culture was saved.

The Sumerian and Egyptian cultures were the direct result of this survival. These cultures could not have grown up so quickly with their mathematical knowledge and astronomical knowledge, far less their ability to build pyramids and maintain great cities. There are far too many "out of place artefacts" for the present establishment view of history, and real history should begin much earlier, before the Flood.

The Earth's sudden pole shift, from the near vertical to the present 23.5 degrees, would account for the disappearance of any civilization then extant. The Biblical account of the flood ties in with the dates, and the evidence should be re-examined in that light. It also accounts for the dramatic change in climate and the disappearance of so many species of mammal. The mammoths found in the frozen tundra of Siberia are evidence to the suddenness of this disaster, as they were found in many cases frozen in the act of eating. At that time, the vast plains of Siberia were temperate and supported huge herds of animals.

The build-up of ice at the poles would take place as the seasons became more pronounced due to the poles being no longer near vertical. This would initiate an ice age as the seasons readjusted to the new pole position. It was in this new world that the survivors had to cope and build a new culture, so there is little surprise that they were handed the title 'cave men' by another culture ignorant of the true facts.

It is also an interesting fact that every culture on earth has a flood legend and a legend containing stories of 'culture-bringers' who arrived from the sea and taught them civilization. It would therefore be wrong of us not to make more of an effort to get to the truth about the vanished civilisation, for in truth, they are our own ancestors.

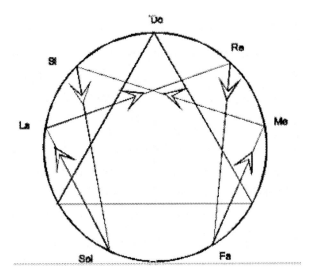

The Enneagram is an ancient Sufi diagram and it also appears in the literature of Freemasonry symbols. The inner triangle represents the 'Eternal or Infinite' aspect of the diagram and yet it is an integral part of the octave around the perimeter, which represents linear time. Therefore the triangle is impinged upon the octave but not part of it in the sense that the triangle represents the infinite aspect and the sounding of doh (ut), as a creative act, entering into the dimension of physical reality.

The inner diagram around the triangle is the inner aspect of linear time and physical reality and is the moving part of the diagram, represented by Re, Me, Fa, Sol, La, recurring. One could say that this is the aspect of the Spirit impinged on physical reality. The two points of the triangle which emerge between Mi/Fa and Sol/La, represent the spiritual influence within physical reality and are the points at which help is available and where the Spiritual

Being can make changes by extra efforts to acquire real esoteric knowledge.

These two points are the places where the spirit interfaces with the physical in a meaningful exchange. This may well be the purpose of the places of power like Rosslyn Chapel and the other sites on the pilgrim route from Compostela. There is much to be studied in the relationship of the inner and outer diagrams and their relationship to the idea of linear time as represented by the octave moving around the circumference of the circle, and how the inner diagram seems to encapsulate linear time and cross over past, present and future by its movement around the diagram.

The outer triangle remains immoveable and seems to take no part in the movements of the inner diagram, but nevertheless initiates the octave and influences the result. In a general way, the whole diagram represents the interplay between the Spiritual and the physical and their relationship one to the other. Finally, it shows the way to spiritual gain and improvement and how to go about it, illustrating that linear time need not be the great problem it appears to be.

Once again, the diatonic scale is at the centre of the Enneagram and it presents another spiritual tool to understanding the hidden influences to which we are exposed every day but which by study and application we could become aware. This was the entire purpose of the early pilgrims who walked the way to spiritual awakening by way of the places of power. Once you depart from the logical mind and its association with the body and physical reality and adopt the infinite aware/conscious mind of the Spiritual Being, then you are stepping into the realm of infinite possibility unhampered by the logical cause-and-effect nature of the logical mind within linear time.

All of the arguments and discussion on the media concerning E.S.P., sixth sense, mysterious happenings, miracles and mysteries, all come about by trying to run these two horses in the same race!

When you adopt the infinite viewpoint, you must abandon the logic and the concept of linear time as such. The 'reasons why' scenario of the logical mind simply does not apply and one of the most difficult things to do is to abandon the 'reasons why' and the 'logical explanation' mind set. This has recently been proved to be the case by new research in quantum physics. If we wish to evolve as Spiritual Beings we have to do just that and adopt the 'all possibilities' mind set of the Infinite Spiritual Being and step out of linear time. At s ource, we are in fact multidimensional beings with the ability to be omnipresent throughout time. That the places of power, and the pilgrimage route to Rosslyn Chapel has survived the ravages of time is proof positive that the ancients knew much more than we give them credit for and a great science perished at the time of the flood.

Chapter 18
The Pilgrims

In attempting to understand what the pilgrims, who came here over thousands of years, were attempting to achieve, then there are so many dots that we have to join to find the full picture.

The essential Spiritual qualities within us are at a 'resonant frequency' with which we can contact the greater and matching frequency that will put us in touch with our higher Source. When we contact the true qualities within us and vibrate at the correct resonant frequency we will be in touch with the Greater and Infinite Source of which we are a part. Then nothing can change that and we have gone through a one-way Spiritual door from which there is no going back. This, I feel, was the aim of the Pilgrimage to Rosslyn and may well be the actual Holy Grail, for a spiritual attainment would far outweigh a mere physical object no matter what its connections. You cannot see a truth of this magnitude and remain as you were—the truth changes everything—the perspective is totally reversed and the world and its values are once again in the correct order.

The 'schism' is a barrier composed of beliefs, content, lies and half-truths which we are born into and which we duplicate, create and go into agreement with, thus becoming divided from our true Selves. There are two viewpoints we can assume to handle this situation—one is to fight our way from the bottom up through all of the lies and content, or we can connect with the higher qualities within us which is part of our Life endowment from the Greater and Infinite Source, thus taking the higher viewpoint and working from the top down in a position of power, to close off the schism.

When we realise that we are responsible for the 'content' we create within us and that all of the content, lies and half truths are duplicated and created by ourselves, then we can simply separate out from them and see them for what they are—our own creations. Then what the right hand has done the left hand can undo. From this viewpoint of power we can see that we create it all for ourselves.

The next step is the most important one: which viewpoint do we assume to handle the situation? Do we attempt to handle it from a tacit agreement that we are creatures of the physical reality attempting to become spiritual beings, or do we assume the viewpoint of a knowing and aware Creator—knowing that we create the content of our mind and our fundamental beliefs and that whatever we create will either be our salvation or our prison bars? It is a great leap from there to the point of taking responsibility for all that goes on within us and to realise we create it all—it is up to us whether we create ourselves as victims or victors! To be able to do this we have to create a bridge between ourselves as we are now and those essential inner qualities that are inherent in our true nature as individual 'drops" from the Greater and Infinite ocean of Beingness from which we arise.

Only then can we take full responsibility for all of it and do it from a condition of power and knowingness.

Chapter 19
Evolution of the Species and the Catalytic Effect

Man is no different from any other species inasmuch as he must evolve, or begin the resulting process of extinction. In this case, the evolution must be a spiritual one if Man is to survive his self-destructive nature of 'evolution by war'. Before we can look at how this will be done, we have to examine Man's present makeup and condition so that we can observe what is required if he is to survive his downward spiral to self-destruction.

Truth can be an elusive commodity, but in this case the truth of the matter is that Man has reached his physical evolutionary goal and must look to his spiritual progress if he is to evolve any further. To do this he has to take a radical view of what he actually IS and what he is not.

For too long he has been educated into believing that he is a body first and foremost—a creature of the physical reality—which could not be further from the truth. Secondly, successive religions have educated him into believing that he is a victim of original sin leaving him with a deep-seated sense of guilt and unworthiness. One has only to take a stroll around any gallery and observe the large medieval religious paintings to get this sense of unworthiness screaming at you from the canvas! This situation, which has lasted for hundreds of years, has been at the root of many destructive religious wars starting with the crusades to the Middle East. Man has to somehow find a way out of this destructive religious loop if he is to regain his true spiritual heritage.

Science and physics are at last coming around to show the way in quantum physics in which a number of advances in recent years, referring to the Zero Point Field, points up the spiritual rather than the physical nature of the universe. The way I have come to see it, is that we are part of a 'super spectrum' of energies all obeying the same basic laws from the basest physical objects, all the way to the spiritual aesthetic wavelengths. However, the important fact is that beyond this point we <u>enter the creative universe of the spirit</u>. For each and every spiritual Being on this planet, this is his or her home universe except that on this 'prison planet' each of us have lost awareness of this fact. The fact of the matter is that the human is first and foremost a spiritual being who **has** a body rather than who **is** a body, and it is from that premise that the matter of the next evolution of the species must take place.

Certain religious dogma has trapped the Being in a mythical belief system, which has caused him/her to abdicate from his true spiritual condition. It sits like a schism or a buffer between the Being and his true Source and bars the way back to his true concept of himself as the Source/Creator in his own inner spiritual space. Once this concept is achieved, the Being will realize that he is the Creator of his own mind, data and pictures and he will cease to be driven obsessively by his mind and its belief systems. When this realization dawns, the Being's viewpoint is reversed through 180 degrees and he is no longer a 'creature of the physical reality' and comes to the realisation that he creates his own world. The freedom from being mind-and belief-driven produces an evolved Being and a new Man, which in turn becomes the first step in the next evolution of the species.

At this point I will introduce the subjects of 'resonance' and the 'collective consciousness'. This is the HOW, where the above is the WHAT.

From the point of view of recent advances in quantum physics, called the 'wave/particle duality', whereas the human being sees himself as particle-based, physics tells us that man (and all matter) is a physical body (particle) but is in fact also a spiritual Being (wave). As a 'wave' in this context, man the individual is also part of the collective consciousness, in touch with it in its entirety. The problem is that man has fallen away from his awareness of himself as a 'wave', in this context, and the next evolution of the species is the recovery of this concept and his 'resurrection' as a spiritual Being.

The 'particle/wave' concept gave me the clue about a new particle in the human collective which is also a wave, and the NEW particle, which has not existed before in the collective, is the next step in the evolution of the spiritual collective consciousness and it will go on as a wave to reach all parts of the collective, and as such it is building a bridge within it for all Beings to cross to the new level of spiritual evolution for the species. It will reach out like a great spider's web to resonate with the entire collective via its wave form (resonant frequency). This new particle will be permeating the collective and building a bridge to the other Beings by 'catalytic proximity' and the resonant wave duality factor of the Beings - this is very much in the nature of the Zero Point Field Theory of modern physics.

All evolution is triggered by a mutation of one member of a species, which is passed to other members of the species by the genes and DNA.

On the subject of a spiritual evolution, the mechanism is slightly different. The mutation is as described above, when a member of the species moves to a higher spiritual vibrational frequency and crosses from creature of the physical reality, to Source/Creator. The Being moves from being a 'particle' to the knowingness of being a 'wave'. This 'wave' condition obeys the law of resonance and in the same way as a physical mutation is passed down to the species by the genes - in the case of the spiritual evolution - it is passed down through the collective consciousness/Zero Point Field via the law of resonance and thus the new frequency vibrational resonance permeates the field, to be matched by those Beings who approximate the source frequency.

In the context of the evolutionary trigger being one member of the species, the whole is the sum of its parts, and it therefore follows that the parts influence the nature of the whole. In this case, the evolved part would have a catalytic effect on the whole via the energy spectrum of the collective consciousness, for the part cannot live in isolation from the whole and must therefore have interaction with it.

In 2005, the NASA science website reported on a mysterious but powerful energy frequency coming from the direction of the center of the galaxy. A spokesman said that it was permeating every atom in the solar system, which would have an effect that, as yet, cannot be predicted. This points up the fact that there are influences at work both within and from without the collective consciousness, for we do not live in a static universe, and I would say that evolution is the norm rather than the exception and that we are all part of an ongoing evolution at this time.

All of this begs the question... is what I have described a reality at this time? It is my belief from my own researches and experience that it is. It has been at work in the collective consciousness and we are probably too close to it to observe it properly, but its effects will become visible as time goes on. Neither are we aware of the unpredictable effects from outside the solar system. But whatever happens, nothing stands still and it is obvious in many ways that we are in a time of dramatic change.

WHISPERS

In Life,
I listen for the whispers.
Those far off voices,
That speak,
Of other times,
And other places.
Of magic and mystery,
That a mundane reality,
Smothers and ignores.

They hint at former splendour,
Or murmur softly,
Of a future,
Bright with promise,
And great purposes,
Yet to be achieved.

I listen for the whispers,
And I am transported,
To the Infinite,
And creative universe,
Of the enchanted Spirit.

Tommy Mitchell

Appendix
The Anatomy of the Diatonic Scale

Music has been at the heart of the human race since day one and the earliest written records of music can be traced back to the early Egyptians. The fact that the mathematics of the diatonic scale are to be found in the ratios which are common to sacred geometry and the symbol *phi*, tells us that it has much greater significance than may have been realised. The ancients used the diatonic scale in their religious and astronomical studies, and it appears in esoteric teachings as the symbol of a ladder to higher spiritual states. The Gurdjieff teaching 'The Work' calls it "the side octave to the sun" and assigns to each note a planet, representing a step in spiritual progress.

The subject of chords and how they arise brought me to the Diatonic scale, and the realisation that in the harmonic sense, music is to a great extent taught, back to front. A student is ploughed into the complexities of the chromatic major/minor system without the advantages of knowing the historical progression from the diatonic system to the Chromatic system. They appear to be taught as two separate entities, rather than one related system. A good analogy is a river, where one can imagine the student setting off against the current in a boat where the river is widest and the current strongest, when in fact he could begin at the source where the river is narrowest and easily managed and where he could 'go with the flow'. The main aim here is to go beyond the simple interpretation of the score to an additional dimension of lending harmonic understanding to your musical arrangements.

This method teaches the subject of harmony and progression using the diatonic scale as the historical starting point of all music. Once you have this concept in mind, the rest will fall into place on a gradient scale from simplicity to complexity, in an easily understood format.

The structure and mathematics of the diatonic scale was developed and perfected in Greek times by Pythagoras. The scale has eight tones composed of two TETRACHORDS.

TETRACHORD :- A series of four Diatonic notes encompassing a perfect fourth. The name comes from the Greek:
Tetra = Four; Chord = String
Each tetrachord is made up of two whole-tone steps (WT), and one half-tone step (HT), resulting in two perfect fourths, making up the eight notes of the scale as shown in the Diatonic Scale diagram..
The 'perfect' intervals or ratios are the perfect fourth, the perfect fifth and the octave.

In the context of DIATONIC HARMONY, the TONIC or KEYNOTE, the FOURTH and the FIFTH are the most important tones in creating Harmonic progressions

The following diagrams show the perfect intervals and ratios of the scale.

PERFECT 4TH AND 5TH AND PRIMARY CHORDS

Fig.1

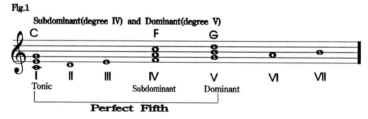

Fig.2

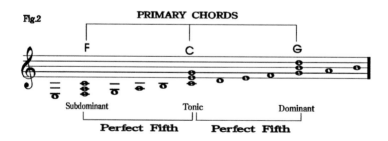

AN INTERVAL IS THE DISTANCE IN PITCH BETWEEN TWO NOTES OF A SCALE.

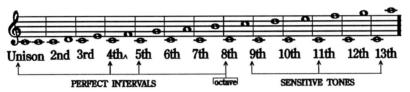

Unison 2nd 3rd 4th∧ 5th 6th 7th 8th 9th 10th 11th 12th 13th

PERFECT INTERVALS   octave   SENSITIVE TONES

Intervals, Scale Tones and the naming of Degrees

Pythagoras, in Greek times, is credited with the development of the Diatonic Scale. He divided the scale into mathematical intervals. Within the scale, the ratio of 2:3 creates a fifth and a ratio of 3:4 creates a fourth. These were designated 'perfect intervals'. The unison and the octave are also perfect interval. Intervals are always calculated from the lowest note to the highest, the lower note counting as the first note.

DIATONIC SCALE - Using eight notes of the musical scale without chromatic variations.

CHROMATIC SCALE - Using all thirteen semitones of the musical scale to obtain chromatic variations. This is achieved by the addition of **five semitones** placed between the whole-tones of the Diatonic Scale.

The following diagram shows the diatonic scale with the additional half-tones inserted between the whole-tones of the scale to obtain the **chromatic scale** consisting of thirteen half-tones (which includes the octave) and which is known today as the major/minor system.

It demonstrates graphically how the evolution of the diatonic scale made it possible to **alter** the scale tones of the diatonic scale to obtain the twelve modern chromatic scales, thus creating the major/minor system, which is much more musically flexible.

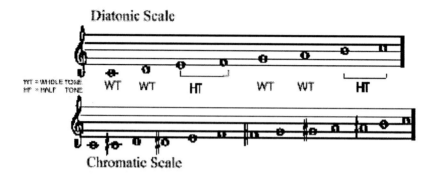

Diatonic Scale

WT = WHOLE TONE
HT = HALF TONE

WT   WT   HT   WT   WT   HT

Chromatic Scale

When I first became interested in the anatomy of the diatonic scale, it was prompted by my curiosity as to why medieval music sounded very different to modern music. The reason is that prior to the evolution of the chromatic thirteen note scale, musical expression was restricted simply because there are only eight notes (including the Octave) in the diatonic scale. This means broadly that you are stuck with seven notes at their given pitch and it is impossible to alter any scale tone from that given pitch. This was compensated for, to some degree by the introduction of the modal system, and this was achieved by transposition of the tonic (Doh/Ut) or keynote. For example by transposing the tonic from C to D, a second scale was created which allowed for variations in the melodic structure of the music.

There are seven modes, each associated with the seven scale tones as follows:
Ionian, Dorian, Phrygian, Lydian, Mixolydian, Aeolian and Locrian.

Each mode allowed a certain flexibility in melodic and harmonic variation, but nevertheless limited the scope of the composer. By the 16th century, music was evolving and the addition of five additional semi-tones between the whole tones of C, D, F, G, and A, (the five black notes on the piano keyboard) revolutionised the scale to produce the 13-note chromatic scale. The result was that any scale tone could be altered by either sharpening or flattening the note and thus allowing melodic and harmonic flexibility which was not possible with the diatonic scale alone. The effect on music in the 17th and 18th centuries is there for all to hear. The greatest innovator was J.S.Bach, who perfected the 'circle of fifths', and gave us a whole new harmonic vista. It has to be noted, however, that despite those advances, the laws and rules of the diatonic scale did not change and remain the corner stone of musical composition.

The Diatonic Scale and the 'Always' Rule

The 'always' rule reflects the fact that on each of the seven notes of the scale, chords can only arise in one form and cannot be altered. It is in fact this rule that sets the recognisable impression that medieval music creates using the diatonic scale and its modes. When referring to a chord on a degree of the scale, it is identified using Roman numerals. The following list shows the chords that arise on each degree of the scale.

> **The I   chord is always major.**
> **The II chord is always minor.**
> **The III chord is always minor.**
> **The IV chord is always major.**
> **The V   chord is always major.**
> **The VI chord is always minor.**
> **The VII chord is always diminished.**

Building four note chords in ascending thirds in the key of C you can see how the chords arise and that they cannot arise in any other way until the additional five semitones are present.

Definitions:

HARMONY :
The study of chords, their nature, use and their progression.
CHORD :
A combination of three or more tones sounded simultaneously.
PROGRESSION :
A harmonically related succession of chords.
INTERVAL :
The distance in pitch between two notes of a scale.

How Chords arise on the Diatonic Scale

Moving horizontally from scale tone to scale tone, 1 to 8, and building vertically in thirds, 1 to 9, we obtain the seven basic chords of the diatonic scale.

These chords can only arise in one way, as shown on the next diagram:

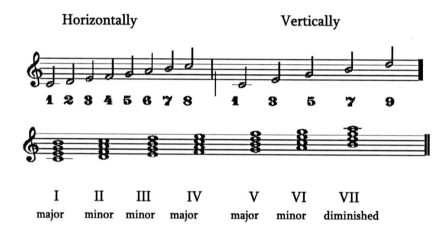

Here we reach the point of having demonstrated the basic anatomy of the diatonic scale and how it is constructed, from the same mathematical ratios as demonstrated by the Fibonacci numbers series, which also applies to the mathematics of sacred geometry and 'music in stone'.

Epilogue

Many threads were pulled together to help me find the music in the cubes, both factual and esoteric, but in the end we are still left with a mystery. That is the mystery of what exactly was in the mind of William St. Clair when he completed the Chapel and secreted the music in the arches. We can always apply our intuition, based on knowledge and experience but it still comes down to the question: was it factual or was it esoteric, or a combination of both?

If it were purely factual, then I would say that the music was placed in the ceiling arches between the pillars for a specific reason. Those who are initiated into Freemasonry find truth beyond the pillars as they pass symbolically into the Temple of Solomon, which represents a blueprint for a new life in the spirit. If it is also esoteric, then the music of the cubes perhaps resonates with that truth and entrains a higher vibrational brain function in the initiates during the initiation ceremony.

Another theory, which led to my choice of a text for the Rosslyn music, is that the music is the lost 'Hymn of John the Baptist', which was banned by the medieval Church. The story goes that many Templars were called 'Johnites', for their belief was that John the Baptist was the true Messiah and that it was he who should fulfil the prophecy. Thus to preserve the hymn, William St. Clair had it carved into the arches as a group of ciphers.

The resonant frequency of the piece of music which is written using the basic diatonic scale, and containing the same mathematics, ratios and proportions as the sacred geometry of the architecture of the building, might be designed to resonate with the building to produce an effect of which we are not aware at this time, but which could be revealed when the music is played in the Chapel. Perhaps my suggestion in chapter 10, that the Grail is in fact the Chapel itself and the truths that it has to offer via the focal point of the music of the cubes, solves the great mystery.

As one mystery is resolved, several others rise to take its place, and so we are invited by the Chapel to continue our endeavours to solve those mysteries, and in the accomplishment of our task, we may acquire much more of the knowledge and truths that it has to offer us.

Tommy Mitchell

BIBLIOGRAPHY

The Field
Lynne McTaggart
Harper Collins Publishers, 2003

The New View Over Atlantis
John Michell
Thames and Hudson, 1983

Universal Laws Never before Revealed
Keely's Secrets
Dale Pond
The Message Company, 2000

The Crystal Sun
Robert Temple
Century London, 2000

The Penguin Encyclopaedia of Ancient Civilizations
Penguin Books, 1980

Psychological Commentaries
Maurice Nicol
Vincent Stuart, London, 1957

Underworld: Flooded Kingdoms of the Ice Age
Graham Hancock
Century

From Atlantis to the Sphinx
Colin Wilson
Virgin Books, 1997

In Search of Atlantis
Rand and Rose Flem-Ath
St Martins Paperbacks, 1997

The Morning of the Magicians
Louis Pauwels and Jacques Bergier
Souvenir Press Ltd, 1960, 2001

Quicksilver Heritage
Paul Screeton
Sphere Books Ltd, 1977

The Stairway to Heaven
Zecharia Sitchin
Harper Collins Publishers, 1983

Entering the Circle
Olga Kharitidi
Harper Collins Publishers, 1996

Pyramid Power
Max Toth & Greg Nielsen
Destiny Books, 1985

Fibonacci series and Phi
Website:
http://goldennumber.net

The Stone Puzzle of Rosslyn Chapel
Philip Coppens
Frontier Publishing/
Adventure Unlimited Press, 2004

INDEX